The Tactical Marksman

A Complete Training Manual for Police and Practical Shooters

100 yds

sports .002
stom
300 W.M. ?

Dave M. Lauck

PALADIN PRESS
BOULDER, COLORADO

D1157244

Other Books by Dave M. Lauck:

The Tactical 1911:
   The Street Cop's and SWAT Operator's Guide
   to Employment and Maintenance

The Tactical Marksman:
A Complete Training Manual for Police and Practical Shooters
by Dave M. Lauck

Copyright © 1996 by Dave M. Lauck

ISBN 0-87364-881-1
Printed in the United States of America

Published by Paladin Press, a division of
Paladin Enterprises, Inc.,
Gunbarrel Tech Center
7077 Winchester Circle
Boulder, Colorado 80301 USA
+1.303.443.7250

Direct inquiries and/or orders to the above address.

Visit our Web site at www.paladin-press.com

Contents

Warning

FIREARMS AND FIREARMS TRAINING ARE POTENTIALLY DANGEROUS AND MUST BE handled responsibly by individual operators. The technical information presented here on training, gunsmithing, and shooting inevitably reflects the author's beliefs and experience with particular firearms, equipment, and components under specific circumstances that the reader cannot duplicate exactly. The information in this book is therefore presented *for academic study only* and should be approached with great caution. Neither the author nor the publisher assumes any responsibility for the use or misuse of information contained in this book.

Firearms possession and use are regulated by the federal Bureau of Alcohol, Tobacco, and Firearms, as well as various state and local statutes. Stiff penalties and possible imprisonment can result from failure to obey these laws. It is *your* responsibility to find out which laws apply before buying or using any firearm.

Acknowledgments

THE AUTHOR WOULD LIKE TO EXTEND SINCERE THANKS TO THE FOLLOWING PEOPLE for their assistance with this project:

• Robert and Janet Finnesey, for their encouragement to begin an ambitious project.
• GMGP
• John Appel, for his expert computer skills and dedication to the project.
• Gary Paul Johnston, Harry Kane, and Harris Publications for their photos, evaluations, and testing of D & L Sports products.
• All of the range assistants for their dedication to monumental range tasks at the D & L Small Arms Training Academy (S.A.T.A.).
• N.T.O.A. and *Tactical Edge* magazine.
• Gale McMillan, for his input and experience with specialized rifle projects.
• Cameron Hopkins, Dave Anderson, Scott Farrel, Ichi Nagata, Layne Simpson, Walt Rauch, Mark Longsdale, the *Soldier of Fortune* magazine staff, and related publications for coverage and evaluation of D & L Sports products.
• Clint Smith of Thunder Ranch and Massad Ayoob of Lethal Force Institute for their support.
• Bruce Massau for his dedication to the art.
• The dedicated D & L Sports clients, who are more than good customers; they're good friends with a mutual interest in performance.
• The staff at Paladin Press, Jon Ford, Karen Pochert, and Donna DuVall, for their insight into the police tactical environment and the need for shooting information directly related to the specific needs of the tactical marksman, as well as their publishing assistance.
• The people who asked not to be mentioned but contributed their special expertise and support to this book.

Preface

THE PRODUCTS AND INFORMATION CONTAINED IN this book are considered state of the art, as of the publication date.

The equipment and techniques discussed in this book have proven reliable under field conditions. New products, and in some cases shooting techniques, are always evolving. The D & L S.A.T.A. is a proving ground for shooters to combine new ideas and equipment in a quest for top performance. New ideas that prove reliable and practical will be incorporated in future writings by me and in the S.A.T.A. training curriculum.

Logo of D & L Small Arms Training Academy.

Introduction

THIS BOOK WAS WRITTEN TO PROVIDE REALISTIC SHOOTING INFORMATION FOR THE reader who wants practical guidelines on "how to" and "what works."

I will attempt to take the shooter past the unscrupulous gun writer's hype for hire and tales of fantastic marksmanship and into the nuts and bolts of what it takes to be a professional marksman. The information contained herein should assist the rifle shooter improve his skills, from point-blank action to extended-range precision firing.

Tactical rifle marksmanship is the primary emphasis of this writing, with a secondary aim of providing information for the practical competition shooter.

This book will not cover the legal ramifications of a defensive firearm encounter. I believe it is the responsibility of the firearm owner to research the rules, regulations, and laws governing defensive use of firearms in his particular area.

Safe, responsible firearms use and ownership will be addressed. You must be willing to make the commitment to serious study and application of safety guidelines before all else.

Safety

IF YOU ARE THE OWNER OF A FIREARM, WHETHER FOR SPORT, DEFENSE, OR SPECIAL operations, you are responsible for its safe handling and storage. The thought of being responsible for a careless death, by your hand or another's, because of a firearm you failed to store properly should be enough incentive to make you constantly aware of and strive for safety.

Firearms themselves are repeatedly blamed for the results of human carelessness and criminal activity. Except for extremely rare cases, assigning blame is just an attempt to escape responsibility for a mistake or criminal conduct. Outside of the general improbability of any mechanical malfunction of the firearm-ammunition combination, you, the weapons operator, have sole control over the safety of the firearm. Following a few basic rules of gun handling and storage can virtually eliminate the so-called accidental discharge. Information in this chapter will help readers understand that the "accidental discharge" is, in reality, a careless or unintentional discharge.

ALL GUNS ARE ALWAYS LOADED

This idea needs to be taken seriously at all times. Provided that it is, the weapon will be handled properly, and there will never be need to claim "I didn't know it was loaded" after a mishap. All guns are always loaded and should always be controlled.

DO NOT LET YOUR MUZZLE COVER ANYTHING
YOU ARE NOT WILLING TO DESTROY

This simple statement says it all. Don't add anything to it, such as, "Don't let the muzzle of your *loaded gun* cover anything you are not willing to destroy." They must never cover anything you are not willing to take the responsibility for destroying. Just because your firearm is not covering anyone in your immediate area does not mean it is not covering anyone in another area or structure. The penetrative

A ready but safe bolt position for target area coverage. Do not lock down unless the situation requires it.

power of a bullet, especially a high-powered rifle bullet, needs to be kept in mind at all times. Safe muzzle control means not covering any undeserving person, including yourself. When you case your rifle or holster your pistol, control your muzzle. When using your long gun and wearing a sidearm, be aware of the muzzle directions of both. A poor sidearm holster selection can position your pistol so that it is pointed at you; and in some rifle-shooting positions, inattention to your holstered pistol's position can lead to covering others in the area, such as the range officer behind the prone firing line.

The tactical marksman must develop a technique for being instantly prepared to fire without violating this or other safety rules. The bolt-action rifle can be fully loaded and kept at the "safe ready" by keeping the bolt handle raised and the firing pin locked in place. The muzzle should be directed to a safe area, and the bolt handle should not be closed until a shot is justified. The fully loaded semiauto rifle can be kept at the ready by activating the manual safety and keeping the muzzle off target in a safe area. Do not *directly* view targets through a mounted rifle scope unless the action is justified. Thoroughly test your equipment to ensure that it will not unintentionally discharge during a hard, fast-bolt lockdown or deactivation of the manual safety. This is especially important under extreme cold conditions where improper lubrication can cause weapons to freeze up.

KEEP YOUR FINGER OFF THE TRIGGER UNTIL YOUR SIGHTS ARE ON THE TARGET AND YOU ARE PREPARED TO FIRE

Having your finger on the trigger before your sights are aligned is an unintentional discharge waiting to happen, especially with a finely tuned rifle trigger. If you are justified in shooting a target, align your sights on the target before placing your finger on the trigger. Until your sights are aligned your shot placement is not confirmed. An unintentional shot could be disastrous. Properly trained shooters develop a trigger finger that operates separately from the grip pressure of the rest of the hand. A well-trained trigger finger is not prone to unintentionally releasing the shot, even when the shooter is startled.

BE SURE OF YOUR TARGET AND WHAT IS BEYOND

This is a simple yet effective statement that all too often goes unheeded. You do not shoot at noises, shadows, or movements. You must identify your target and confirm a safe backstop behind your target before firing. For the tactical marksman in a hostage situation, for instance, this may be an exacting task: hostage takers using disguises and/or live shields can make this extremely difficult at times. Nevertheless, the rule must be adhered to. On occasion, the tactical marksman will have to adjust his position to ensure a safe backstop—as in increasing the angle of the shot to use the ground as a backstop. Increasing the angle of the shot and the difficulty of the shot's calculation require advanced training to guarantee proper performance.

ALWAYS WEAR YOUR SAFETY EQUIPMENT

Eye and ear protection are a must while shooting. Your shooting glasses should be made out of shatter-resistant material. Quality glasses will not only provide protection while firing, but they will also give some protection should you be fired upon. If an adversary decides to search your area by fire, quality eye protection will reduce damage from secondary projectiles.

The lenses should be distortion-free when they are looked through from any angle (some glasses will have distortion at severe angles, such as in prone shooting at high angles). The frame should also be unobtrusive so that it will not interfere with top and side vision. Strength, comfort, and low reflectivity are all extremely important considerations. Blind shooters will have problems completing their missions. *Wear your glasses.*

Ear protection has always been a problem for the tactical marksman, who must be alert to his surroundings and communications, yet must protect his hearing. The best development in this area is electronic earplugs. These inside-the-ear devices protect your ears from harsh noise, enhance your ability to hear low-level sounds, and outperform electronic muffs because the plugs are less cumbersome and allow proper head-to-stock positioning.

Always wear personal safety equipment during live fire and carry first-aid supplies in your gear.

Entry team personnel will also benefit from these high-tech hearing protectors. Enhanced hearing with instant shutdown/turn-on works well for explosive and flash-bang entries, not to mention eager teammates who fire beside your head.

The drawback, as with other quality equipment, is the price, which is approximately $500 per set. In addition, the earplugs have to be individually form-fitted by a professional.

DRUGS AND ALCOHOL DO NOT MIX WITH FIREARMS

Though this should be obvious, the rule is often ignored. An unintentional discharge from the firearm of a shooter who is under the influence of drugs or alcohol will not give him a legal leg to stand on in the event of damage to persons or property. Any tactical unit on 24-hour call, for example, should have a standing order of no drug or alcohol consumption at any time. A tactical officer who reports for duty knowing that he has consumed alcohol or drugs (including any legally prescribed or over-the-counter medication that impairs judgment or reflexes) must be responsible enough to immediately report the information to the commander and worry about the consequences later.

DO NOT LEAVE YOUR WEAPON UNATTENDED

You are responsible for the security of your firearms. Unsecured firearms have led to the wounding or death of many children and the gain of many criminals. If you are not in direct control of your firearm, it should be under lock and key. Glass display cases, including the rear windows of pickup trucks, are not secure; get a secure vault.

If you are a tactical officer, ensuring that your equipment is secured is not merely a question of safety. Any time your equipment is out of your direct control, you cannot be confident that it is undisturbed: curious or destructive personnel may tamper with your equipment while you are not present. This means that anytime you are away from your unsecured equipment, you must examine it and confirm the zero before its duty use.

ASSIGN A QUALIFIED RANGE OFFICER

Shooting takes concentration, and dangerous situations developing at the range may go undetected by the occupied shooter. A competent range officer is able to detect unexpected range developments, such as a person appearing in the impact area, before problems occur. The range officer can also assist with any medical emergencies or injuries the lone shooter may otherwise incur.

SELECT A PROPER RANGE

Your range selection must be suitable for the firearms you are shooting. A positive backstop is a must. Range targets, especially now that steel targets are popular, must be suited to the firearm you are using. Damaged steel targets may cause serious bullet fragments, which can spatter back at persons on the range.

DO NOT SACRIFICE SAFETY FOR ANY ADVANTAGE

Do not cut corners on safety procedures in an attempt to gain a shooting edge. This is especially true with equipment modifications, such as trigger-pull adjustments. Excessively light, unreliable trigger engagements are completely unsuitable for tactical missions. Gun-handling techniques that violate safety rules in a quest for more speed must not be used. Unsafe ammunition, no matter what spectacular performance is claimed for it, must not even be considered.

KNOW YOUR EQUIPMENT

Fully understanding your equipment will allow you to recognize any emerging problems and apply the proper preventive maintenance. You must be familiar with your equipment and its operation to the point that you can operate in the dark with it. Lack of familiarity with your equipment can cause serious lag time when quick operation is required. Placing your shots correctly is only a matter of luck if you don't fully understand your equipment. Don't base your mission on luck.

AMMUNITION SAFETY

Rifle ammunition should be of the highest quality available and consistently the same for training, duty, or match use. Improperly manufactured ammunition can be extremely unsafe, especially in high-pressure rifle cartridges. Unless you are a professional precision handloader, stay with new factory-loaded match ammunition. All cartridges, whether factory- or handloaded, should be gauged, weighed, and inspected prior to duty carry. Specific ammunition is part of your shooting system: it must remain consistent to keep your performance from varying drastically. Maintain strict control over your ammunition lots.

MALFUNCTIONS AND SAFETY

There is a reason for every malfunction. If your firearm malfunctions regularly and you don't know the cause, have it inspected by a competent armorer. Your firearms should be proven reliable before you take them on duty carry: this does not mean someone telling you that the firearm works. Any time your weapon is out of your control, such as for an armory inspection, carefully examine, test-fire, and rezero it when you get it back.

Malfunctions on a mission can be disastrous, and they are compounded by improper clearance procedures. Do not try to fire through barrel obstructions. There should be no need to forcibly operate your weapon if proper clearance procedures are used. If you are well trained in your firearm's operation, safely clearing stoppages should be a simple task. Should you become a victim of Murphy's Law, be prepared to make a fluid transition to your support (backup) weapon.

• • •

Good safety habits will become second nature if they are always observed. Safe habits are extremely important in high-stress encounters; unintentionally shooting yourself or your partner will do little to help you survive the mission.
Make safety a habit at all times!

The Tactical Marksman Concept

THE TERM *TACTICAL MARKSMAN,* AS USED IN THIS BOOK, REFERS TO A POLICE OFFICER assigned to a special response team, not a military sniper. There are wide differences between the roles of the police marksman and the military sniper.

The military sniper often simply shoots targets of opportunity in wartime. He is less likely to be involved in situations where there are hostages or innocent bystanders; he rarely has to consider the civil liability that regularly confronts a police tactical marksman. A police response team always has to act under an authorized use-of-force policy, making positive identification of the target, protecting the safety of others in the area, and being able to justify any action taken. Such requirements, of course, narrow the scope of situations and ranges in which a tactical marksman can prudently fire.

The additional responsibilities of police marksmen also dictates higher standards than those of military snipers. These standards will require a hugely disproportionate amount of time dedicated to training when compared to the amount of time actually spent on call-outs. Maintaining consistently high standards will also be expensive in terms of ammunition and equipment. This is a fact of operation that must be understood by police administrators when placing a marksman team on call. Any police administration that wants an on-call marksman team must be fully committed to the support of the program, or not have one at all. Equipping officers with rifles, even state-of-the-art rifles, does not make them marksmen. Calling on a department's untrained but reputed "best shot" in a crisis could result in serious liability for ill-considered action; a police marksman operates in such a critical area of law enforcement that a mistake can easily result in an unintentional death. His training for and approach to being a marksman must be fully professional because surgical-like precision may be required to resolve a situation with hostiles and hostages in close proximity to each other.

Both military snipers and police marksmen are responsible for observation, intelligence gathering, and reporting. Personnel occupying sniper/marksman positions often serve as the forward eyes and ears of the commander. Accurate, detailed reporting of information is essential to assist the commander in formulating the best plan of action.

To meet the taxing requirements of situations in which marksmen are used, two-man teams are often deployed. The team's job is to protect the innocents, contain the situation, gather intelligence, and report any developments as they occur. Important information that should be gathered by the team would include, but is not limited to, the following: currently observed situations and any changes in same; suspect and hostage descriptions; information about the structure (e.g., windows, doors); approach and escape routes; guard dogs; alertable animals; surrounding terrain and structures; observed weapons; fields of fire available to a suspect; fortifications, booby traps, alarms, or alerting devices; propane or fuel tanks; power sources; telephone lines; portable phone introduction locations; and gas delivery points.

A *marksman-observer team*, in its most literal meaning, provides only one marksman and an observer/assistant. This may be a step above the lone marksman's being expected to fulfill all the required responsibilities of a marksman's post, but it is not as practical as a *two-man marksman team*. Both men on this team should be fully equipped and trained to function as marksman and observer. They should be compatible in personality and physical capability to minimize conflicts and allow either to carry the other in case of injury.

Having the post occupied by two equally trained and proficient marksmen allows for more effective post operation and a more detailed post log. Both team members can share the responsibilities of the post, thus enabling the team to maintain its alertness and readiness more effectively by the alternation of the main rifle position between the two team members. This allows, for example, the two post members to relieve eyestrain caused by high-magnification observation. Trading off positions must not mean trading off on a single rifle, however. Rifles should be issued individually to marksmen, who should use only the rifle with which they are intimately familiar and formally qualified.

The security of the post is also enhanced by double occupancy. The observer can act as close-to-medium-range security with his support carbine and deter any surprise approach. On long-term operations, with no relief available, the two-man post is able to incorporate sleep shifts more safely than those with only a single marksman.

Most situations require multiple marksmen or team positions to cover the area and to improve the chances of a clear shot. A unit commander should allow experienced marksmen to choose and coordinate their own positions in order to provide their own post security and fields of fire; this provides the best "shot-setting" positioning and situation coverage. Team positions selected by command personnel who may not be attuned to what is required for a successful shot may put the team in an impossible position.

The most obvious requirement of a tactical marksman is consistently accurate shooting, but it is not the only requirement. Unfortunately, there has been a noticeable, and disturbing, trend toward more and more wannabes on tactical teams—officers who think that being on such teams makes them special. This type of officer looks forward to attending tactical school pool parties in full ninja regalia and thinks he is competent just because he has been selected and equipped. Aside from the fact that looking neat does not translate into performing well, the pool-party commando rarely has the dedication to be a long-term tactical team member.

For the position of police tactical marksman, a logical mind and stable personality are required. A person who makes decisions based on emotion rather than logic is unreliable as a marksman. A potential tactical marksman must be an intelligent evaluator of potentially high-risk situations; candidates should have demonstrated acceptable decision-making and action-taking ability in past assignments.

The marksman candidate should be his own worst critic, always striving to do better. He will probably be exposed to some new-wave, positive-reinforcement trainers who treat him as a nonthinker, telling him that the world is positive and that the shot he just missed was actually a positive experience, one of which he should be proud. (Often the new-wave trainer comes from a basic 40-hour shooting course and has miraculously become an instant instructor with no other shooting experience.) The ideal candidate will be able to separate the wheat from the chaff—and the truth from trendy training philosophies—and will be oriented toward performance rather than theory.

People who live their lives under adverse conditions can become amazingly resistant to hardship and actually get stronger as they overcome adversity. Street people, addicts, and mentally ill subjects often live hard lives. Police who deal with them often notice how healthy and fit they are in spite of the drug use, poor nutrition, and bad living conditions. The old adage that "that which does not kill you makes you stronger" seems true about these people. On the other hand, modern technology is pushing police officers into a more sedentary life-style through the use of computers, radios, motorized patrols, and increased classroom instruction. Long hours of nonphysical activity, high stress, poor diet, and shift work result in reduced fitness. It takes dedication to overcome all the pressures and temptations to become a "push-button cop" and to maintain a high level of physical fitness. Tactical officers should have this dedication.

Know-it-all veteran officers, who believe that their experience should exempt them from training, make poor tactical marksman. Experience is a great asset, but training must be maintained. Overconfident, "badge-heavy" officers with the attitude that there are only two kinds of people in the world—"pukes and police"—make poor tactical officers. Confidence is a necessary component of the job, but it must be based on performance, not just ego. Black ninja suits leak blood, too, especially if your opponent knows the program. Officers with the "them versus us" attitude miss out on the wealth of knowledge from nonpolice personnel, and knowledge can be critical in operations. Black pajamas and high-capacity 9mms are not the realistic solution to every problem.

A marksman must strive to be professional, not a department "ladder climber" looking for rank or status. Officers with a hidden agenda of personal career advancement do not mesh well with officers dedicated to, and satisfied with, frontline protection for citizens.

There is a situation even worse than that of officers who try to use their tactical status to achieve career gain: politicians who use police operations as stepping-stones to stardom. Self-promoting administrators often place being politically correct in the eyes of the media over employing safe, commonsense tactics. Such spineless administrators commonly adopt a wait-and-see attitude once tactical operations are under way: if all goes well, they gladly accept all the credit; if operations are botched or get critical press, they lie about their involvement and try to direct blame elsewhere. These "sell out the troops" type of administrators often cause officers to have delayed reactions in critical incidents because of concerns about lack of support. Rank in modern law enforcement does not necessarily mean integrity.

Police administrators typically operate in one of two configurations: (1) a pyramid with the chief at the top looking out for his career and his inner circle of friends, an arrangement where rolling shit downhill is the normal method of self-preservation, or (2) the preferred method for line and tactical officers, an inverted pyramid where administrators realize that citizen protection and service is the backbone of police work. These administrations structure all support operations to assist the grunt officers. At the bottom of this pyramid is the true leader, who is ready to support the ethical actions of his troops. All officers should evaluate the configuration their agency employs before committing to the tactical unit.

Frontline troops must have confidence in their administrators to work effectively, so hidden personal and political agendas have no place in tactical operations. The selection committee for new team personnel should be made up of experienced tactical operators who make decisions based on performance—not shiny shoes, smooth talk, and asskissing. Team commanders should come from this same vein of proven performers. Top-quality personnel are the key to a successful team; without them, all the high-tech equipment and ninja suits in the world won't pull the unit through tough operations.

Furthermore, personnel selection staff members must keep in mind the financial investment to be made in any officer chosen. The officer must be dedicated to the long-term mission; the department will lose its training investment if he doesn't work out.

Keep performance as your main requirement for team selection. Allowing the personality element to creep into the selection process will dilute performance. Be prepared for the departmental personalities who will stop at nothing to destroy what they don't have the ambition or skill to be part of. Aggressive administrative action may be required to quell those determined to undermine serious departmental programs.

The tactical officer personality may be a step apart from the general police officer, and the tactical marksman a step beyond the tactical officer. Dedicated precision marksmen are often perfectionists, always learning and improving. Don't discount a marksman as a team player because he would rather continue training alone than go for pizza with the entry team. Precise shooting from a distance requires more range work than 15-yard MP-5 training. The aloof tactical marksman may be the ultimate team player: he is dedicated to extra training to protect his team as well as citizens.

Being a marksman can be physically taxing. Missions frequently require a marksman to move long distances over difficult terrain, with heavy loads. Or, at the other extreme, the marksman might have to endure long periods in a stationary position while observing through high-magnification optics. To perform best in both these situations a marksman must be physically fit. He should not smoke or drink. Ideally, his eyesight should be excellent uncorrected; however, if someone with corrected eyesight is selected, he must be aware of, and prepared for, such problems as lens reflection and loss of or damage to eyeglasses (matte, nonreflective glasses should be mandatory, and at least two extra sets should always be available).

A potential candidate should be required to demonstrate acceptable shooting skills in a controlled range environment as well as his post skills in live situations before he is put on call-out status. This is best accomplished by teaming the candidate with an experienced marksman in situations that allow showing his skills. For example, once he is properly trained and equipped, the tactical marksman should be able to perform to sub-minute of angle (MOA) standards out to at least 300 yards (MOA is a unit of angular measurement equal to 1.047 inches per 100 yards) without assistance. The marksman expected to cover longer ranges (e.g., at airports, in rural flatlands, or during countersniper operations) needs the correct training, equipment, and capabilities for long-range performance. In live situations, the marksman should not fire beyond his demonstrated capabilities.

Personal motivation is an important consideration for potential marksmen, which includes not only the motivation to train, but also that of applying for the position in the first place. A psychological evaluation can help weed out candidates with the wrong ideas about being marksmen before training begins, thereby saving a department time and money and averting possible disgrace or tragedy.

A competent, professional officer who maintains his skills normally translates into a tactical officer who won't overreact in critical situations. Officers should enjoy the tactical challenge: outwitting the perpetrator and ending the situation with a safe, nonviolent arrest. The more violence prone the perpetrator, the more challenging the situation.

Rifle Selection

I BELIEVE IN THE CONCEPT OF "THE RIGHT TOOL FOR THE JOB." THEREFORE, DETERMINING THE proper rifle depends on the task's requirements.

The right equipment for the varmint shooter is obviously not going to work for the big-game hunter. What is best for the bench-rest shooter may not be practical for the tactical marksman. Close-and-quick requirements will be different from far-and-precise ones. A combination of equipment from several categories may be required to achieve realistic field performance. The following information emphasizes equipment best suited for the tactical marksman, but various portions should be of interest to a variety of shooting disciplines.

A police patrol officer, an action shooter, and an inner-perimeter tactical officer may have similar requirements when it comes to rifle selection. All these shooters would benefit from a light, fast-handling carbine that features reliability, light recoil, good accuracy, and compact size. This carbine should be adaptable for both daylight and darkness.

The ranges encountered by the patrolman, action shooter, and perimeter marksman seldom exceed 200 yards, and probably will be much less. In all cases, quick, accurate shots on target are important. Choosing the proper rifle, action, caliber, and sight helps to accomplish this goal.

Scope-sighted rifles have proven more desirable than those with iron sights for achieving top performance. Placing the scope's reticle and the target on the same focal plane eliminates time-consuming iron-sight alignment problems, and the scope sight works better in low-light conditions than iron sights and provides superior target identification. Realizing that the rifle-scope combination could be subjected to rigorous conditions, you must give the scope an added measure of protection. Solid mounting, multiple rings, quality construction, and rubber armoring help achieve this. I have yet to be involved in a mission where a properly mounted, top-quality optic has been rendered unserviceable because of abuse. Obviously Murphy could change this perfect record. I have developed a quick-detachable (QD) iron-sight set and backup scope concept for those who wish to be wise and prepare for the worst. I prefer a prezeroed, preringed scope identical to the one on the rifle to be carried in a protective tube in a backpack. A

Quick-detachable scope mounting and backup iron sights.

damaged scope can be removed and a backup scope attached in less than a minute. Having the scope already prezeroed and tested means that you have only to confirm final zero before getting the rifle back into action.

In my opinion, the semiauto action best fills the midrange carbine needs. The semiauto is simple to operate, which frees the shooter to concentrate on the situation at hand. Actions requiring frequent reloading or action manipulation require more of the operator's attention. Lever actions, pump actions, unnecessarily long magazines, and extra-high scope mounting do not allow the shooter to maintain the best covered position while firing, because they require more room for manipulation and sighting. A low-scoped semiauto can be fired with ease through a 4-inch break in cover, thus making you a much smaller target.

The quality semiauto action, with a properly fitted match barrel, provides excellent accuracy at the distances for which the midrange carbine was designed.

The accuracy of the midrange carbine must be taken into consideration along with other requirements (i.e., handling, compactness, penetration, maneuverability, expected shooting positions, and weight). Rifles can be produced with even more accuracy than the sub-MOA, semiauto, midrange carbine, but the heavier, slower action rifle would not be as practical as the carbine at close to middle ranges. Again, it's a matter of the right tool for the job.

The professional perimeter rifle specifically designed by the author to be used for encounters beyond effective pistol cartridge range in environments not suited to a heavy rifle/cartridge. It has compact, self-contained lights capable of illumination in low-light conditions.

To attain realistic field performance, you must train to overlap the capabilities of your tools to best fit developing situations. Penetration may necessitate a heavy rifle at close range; whereas rifle availability may require an extended hit from your midrange carbine. Proper application of the two-rifle concept allows you to do both.

You should base caliber selection on readily available, top-quality ammunition suited to the job at hand. Two popular caliber selections for the midrange carbine are 5.56mm and 7.62x39mm. Both cartridges are available in a variety of loadings to meet most midrange requirements. Pistol calibers and .30 carbine are popular cartridges for the lightweight carbine, but they lack a suitable trajectory for the long side of the midrange requirements. The .308 Winchester (7.62x51mm) cartridge is more in the battle- or bolt-rifle arena and is a bit on the heavy side in both recoil and semiauto rifle weight. Both of these concerns detract from the superquick deployment of the rifle.

The .308 Winchester is a good choice in a compact semiauto if your needs dictate the more powerful cartridge and if you can handle it quickly. Officers required to operate in dangerous-game environments obviously would want to evaluate the more powerful cartridges. I have found that the benefits of the faster handling, accurate carbine in a lighter caliber outweigh those of the more powerful cartridge in tactical situations, provided that glass or barrier penetration is not required. For most shooters, the lighter carbine, chambered for a medium cartridge, can

QD light mounts can be fitted to long guns and handguns for low-light operations.

The compact, lightweight bolt-action performs well as a general-purpose rifle, but the tactical officer's mission is better served by the semiauto carbine at moderate ranges and the true precision rifle at longer ranges.

Submachine guns and carbines chambered in pistol calibers are quick and accurate at closer ranges but lack the trajectory of the 5.56mm. Penetration of normal building materials is actually less with frangible 5.56mm bullets than with heavier pistol/submachine bullets.

deliver rounds on close- to medium-range, uncovered targets accurately and more quickly than a heavier caliber rifle. Furthermore, correct shot placement with a medium cartridge provides results without as much overpenetration concern as that of a heavier cartridge.

The accuracy and trajectory I have obtained from factory 7.62x39mm rounds out of a semiauto carbine suggest this is not the best carbine-cartridge combination.

The 5.56mm cartridge has proved to be an accurate, reliable choice in midrange carbines. The high-velocity 5.56mm is certainly not a rhino-rolling cartridge, but rolling rhinos is not the job at hand. Quick, accurate shot placement at moderate ranges, most likely to occur in an inhabited environment, is.

When selecting 5.56mm ammunition, remember that the bullet weight should be suited to the rifle you will be shooting. There are numerous barrel-twist rates available in factory rifles, and the rates should be matched with the proper ammunition—drastic differences in accuracy can occur when combining various twist rates and bullet weights.

In 5.56mm, twist rates of 1 turn in 12 to 14 inches are ideal for bullets in the 52- to 55-grain category. A twist rate of 1 turn in 9 inches will handle most bullets from 55 to 69 grains; a rate of 1 turn in 7 inches is more suited to bullets in the longer, heavier range, 62 to 69 grains. Best accuracy results from spinning the bullet just enough to stabilize it.

Longer, heavier bullets need more spin to remain stable in flight. Without proper stabilization, bullet tumbling results, thereby creating unpredictable impact points. Ammunition must be thoroughly tested in the firearms it will be used in before adoption. The 5.56mm ammo currently recommended by me in semiauto police carbine is Federal Premium 55-grain Nosler ballistic tip. The pointed, cannelured bullet gives excellent feeding reliability and accuracy. Overpenetration is not normally a problem, as the ballistic tip usually fragments on impact. Shooters needing .223 penetration with minimal fragmentation should evaluate the Federal .223 tactical load.

The recoil impulse and the weight of 5.56mm ammunition are light and allow for rapid multiple-target or follow-up shots. The magazine capacity allows you to concentrate on shooting rather than counting rounds and reloading. Magazine capacity should not be your first requirement and should not be taken to extremes. As a tactical marksman, you do not need 40-round box magazines and 90-round drums; 20- or 30-round box magazines provide enough of a reservoir to preclude constant reloading, as well as allowing you to use proper firing positions. Magazines that extend too far below the receiver often interfere with proper positioning and use of cover. Such oversized magazines are more prone to reliability problems as well. All magazines for duty use must be proven reliable before being put "on call." Professional marksmen do not fall victim to the "spray and pray" mentality often precipitated by large magazine capacities and semiauto actions.

The goal of a professional marksman is to hit and incapacitate the correct target or targets. In situations that require multiple quick hits, the semiauto action and plentiful ammunition help, but you must remain a disciplined precision shooter. A professional marksman uses rapid fire only when it is required and only to the point that he can control it. A person who uses undisciplined blasting simply because he has a large-capacity magazine should not be a tactical marksman. You should adhere to the one-shot, one-hit theory.

To sum up, quality 5.56mm ammunition gives excellent accuracy and a point-blank range that covers the most realistic ranges for the midrange cartridge/carbine combination. Given that there are many readily available, midrange 5.56mm semiauto carbines, your selection should be based on reliability, accuracy, and practicality.

I have experimented extensively with all the following rifles.

RIFLE MODELS

HK 93 5.56mm

This rifle has proved to be reliable and robust, capable of sub-3 MOA accuracy. It has three primary drawbacks: (1) scope mounting tends to be high above the boreline, (2) the iron sights are marginal (ring apertures on both front and rear sights are of limited value in low-light conditions), and (3) the manual safety lever is difficult to reach from a shooting grip with small- and average-sized hands. The size and weight of the HK-93 are closer to that of a 7.62mm battle rifle than a carbine. The HK 53 is basically a HK 93 reduced to near MP 5 dimensions and provides for a rugged, compact 5.56mm carbine. The select-fire HK 53 is a Class III weapon (full-auto capable), making it difficult to acquire for civilians, and it still suffers from the standard sighting problems.

RUGER MINI-14

The Mini-14 is available in 5.56mm (and the Mini-30 is available in 7.62x39mm). This comparatively inexpensive carbine is lightweight and compact, and has a host of aftermarket accessories of questionable value. In my experience, the Ruger's accuracy, ruggedness, and reliability have been unacceptable, and the aftermarket doodads, many of which are worthless, do not bring this rifle up to an acceptable standard.

M14

The .308 M14 has a substantial following among match shooters because it can be mechanically accurized. The standard M14 stock design is a poor choice in a full-auto version because of poor controllability. The action requires the scope platform to be side-mounted, and mount rigidity has been a problem. Top-ejected cases can be wedged under the mount, and the sightline tends to be too high for a good cheek weld.

ARMALITE 180

The Armalite 180 is available in 5.56mm, with folding stock and 20-inch barrel. The Armalite 18 is available in a more compact select-fire version. The rifles feature a rotating bolt and a dual-operation spring system; they are lightweight and feature welded sheet metal construction. The ruggedness of the magazine latch and folding stock of this rifle are both questionable. The standard scope mount is unacceptable. My experience has been that these rifles are reliable but not very accurate—around 3 MOA at best.

STEYR AUG

The Steyer AUG 5.56mm carbine.

I have tested the 5.56mm AUG bullpup-style carbine a lot. The testing has been limited to two new, personally owned AUGs. Contrary to other reports, my experience with the AUG has been a disappointment. Out-of-the-box accuracy with quality ammunition has been good, but reliability has not. A factory-certified AUG repairman's repeated attempts to fix the problems have failed, and it is my opinion that this rifle is not suitable for duty use. At the least, shooters should thoroughly test-fire it prior to duty use. The Austrian army and many shooters obviously do not share my opinion.

The standard-issue 1.5x integral scope sight is not suitable for precision shooting without reticle replacement. The standard-issue reticle is simply a thick circle that engulfs most of a man-sized target at as few as 300 yards and has no precise aiming point. The replacement reticle with a fine cross hair or dot is better for precision fire. Better yet is a replacement upper receiver that allows for mounting additional types of scopes. More magnification beyond the 1.5x is needed for positive target identification and shot placement at middle ranges. The standard-issue AUG scope sight is rugged, clear, and suitable for standard, less than precise military engagements. The bullpup configuration ejects cases through the side of the stock away from the shooter's cheek weld. Obviously, switched-shoulder shooting can result in cases being ejected into the shooter's face. Negatives include cost and poor trigger pull.

FN FNC

The FN FNC is offered in 5.56mm and has about the same pros and cons as the HK 93. It has almost the same weight and size of a 7.62mm and a stout military trigger pull. On the plus side, it is robust and reliable. Accuracy has typically been in the 3 MOA range.

The big brother to the FNC, the FN FAL in .308 Winchester, is a good choice in a full-sized .308 semiauto or select-fire rifle, which is ideal when a more powerful rifle is required. The semiauto FN FAL is reliable and capable of 2 MOA accuracy with proper ammunition. The full-sized FAL also allows for low scope mounting and good trigger work. The standard-stocked FAL, which differs from the folding-stock paratrooper model, has low felt recoil and good handling characteristics. Marksmen who supplement their preci-

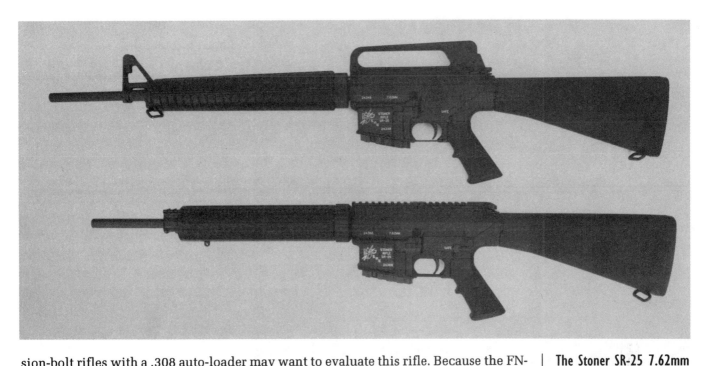

sion-bolt rifles with a .308 auto-loader may want to evaluate this rifle. Because the FN-FAL, like the AR-15, is plagued by poor-quality aftermarket copies, you should choose quality over price to achieve proper performance.

The Stoner SR-25 7.62mm semiautomatic is worth consideration for tactical officers who work in areas that dictate a more powerful weapon.

STONER SR-25

Reed Knight's new SR-25 7.62mm semiauto rifles may also deserve consideration by shooters looking for a 7.62mm. This product is relatively new, however, and needs thorough evaluation.

COLT AR-15 AND SPORTER RIFLES

Colt offers a variety of 5.56mm models in its semi-auto rifle line and has recently offered the "Sporter" rifle in 7.62x39mm. The new Sporters are available in the heavy-barreled, 20-inch Sporter H-Bar, medium-

A custom-built AR-15 is available in numerous configurations and features a variety of options to suit various situations.

Top and middle: Custom tactical AR rifles. Bottom: Released in 2000, the MR-30PG (Marksman's Rifle, .30 caliber, Professional Grade) was designed by the author to be the most field-rugged, accurate tactical rifle available.

barreled, 20-inch Sporter, and 16-inch-barreled, lightweight carbine. Colt has just introduced a "competition" model Sporter with removable carrying handle. These rifles are basically the same as the AR-15, but without the bayonet lug.

• • •

Reviewing the guidelines of the midrange carbine will indicate which model is best for you. If reliability, accuracy, and practicality for close-quarters to medium-range firing are your primary considerations, a full-sized battle rifle is not your best choice.

The Colt H-Bar, with correct ammunition, gives approximately 2 MOA accuracy out of the box, but the extra size and weight hamper fast handling in close action. The 20-inch medium-barreled Sporter has a lighter weight barrel but still has the full length and less than precise accuracy. The competition model also suffers from the full-length heavy barrel and lack of maneuverability, as does the H-Bar, but it does attempt to address the high-sight line problems. The removable handle and rear sight of the competition model permit short-scope mounting to the flat top receiver. The main problem with mounting a scope to the competition model's flat top receiver is that it is either too high, too low, or unsupported. The short, flat top mounting area does not allow for forward scope-tube support of longer scope tubes. Direct scope-ring mounting to the flat top receiver places the scope too low for quick eye positioning. To offset this, Colt supplies a mounting adapter along with the competition model. The adapter mounts to the flat top receiver, and the rings attach to the adapter. The scope then attaches to the rings. This adds an unnecessary complication and places the scope almost as high above the boreline as if the scope were mounted on the handle. This creates an unacceptable trajectory for the midrange shooter who must shoot quickly from point-blank to middle ranges without taking time for trajectory compensations. I have been able to add a rugged rail mount to the competition model's flat top and achieve the proper scope support and height for shooters who have obtained this model, as well as all other models.

There is a great advantage to properly low-scoping your midrange carbine. With a properly zeroed 5.56mm trajectory, you can get a dead-on sight hold from 0 to 225 yards on all but the

The custom-built, low-scoped 5.56mm carbine is my first choice for medium-range tactical situations.

smallest of targets (except for wind-drift compensation). When a carbine scope is low mounted to the correct height, the shooter enjoys proper cheek weld, eye relief, and unstrained neck. The properly set-up carbine yields fine practical accuracy, as well as the above-mentioned benefits, all in a package not much bigger than a submachine gun.

The Colt Sporter lightweight, or carbine, is one factory rifle that comes close to meeting the requirements of the professional's midrange needs. It is reliable, lightweight, and compact. Its drawbacks are the high sightline, poor trigger, and light

contour nonfloated barrel that can be easily affected by handguard pressure. Aftermarket barrel-mounted accessories can also cause the light contour barrel to drastically shift bullet impact. The lightweight Sporter is similar to the CAR-15, except that the Sporter has a fixed buttstock. The collapsible buttstock model has recently been restricted to law enforcement sales only.

The AR-15 Sporter design features a large, single operating spring, rotating bolt, and direct gas operation. The straight-line stock and recoil direction produce rapid fire with minimal muzzle lift. The configuration of the rifle lends itself well to fast operation and handling. The manual safety, magazine release, magazine well, and pistol-grip-to-trigger area are all well designed and located. The quality manufacture of the AR-15 leads to a reli-

Slow-fire precision and rapid-fire follow-up shots are available with the custom "gas gun."

Rugged rail mount from D & L Sports.

Single- or double-compact light mounting on the custom AR-15 extends its nighttime range to more than 100 yards.

D & L AR-15s with and without muzzle brake.

able rifle. There is a "buyer beware" market for AR-15s because of the many inferior after-market copies. Buy the best the first time.

The AR-15's high sight-line problem can be eliminated by machining off the standard high sight bases and carrying handle, and then rigidly installing a rail mount of proper height and length on the receiver. A correctly designed rail base gives enough height for proper eye positioning, yet still maintains an excellent point-blank trajectory and supports the entire length of the scope tube.

The rugged rail mount accommodates a variety of popular ring-scope combinations, including night-vision sighting devices. The AR-style rifle with a low rail mount accepts almost any sighting device with Weaver-style attachments. This includes peep or ghost-ring iron sights suitable for replacing a damaged scope under field conditions.

Barrel flexing and point-of-impact shift can be cured by free-floating the barrel through a custom handguard. The same handguard allows mounting of auxiliary lighting or a laser. Compact handguard-mounted lights allow you to achieve "daytime" accuracy at more than 100 yards at night, without being obtrusive. A bipod can also be mounted on a free-floating handguard without changing the point of impact (POI). Bipods are normally reserved for the full-sized ARs and precision rifles, but can be occasionally useful on the carbines as well. Short-range/long-wait situations can be more easily handled with a bipod-mounted carbine.

I have also added the popular D.L. sling system to the free-floated handguard. In situations that don't allow solid rifle support, the D.L. sling adds great stability.

The same sling, adjusted for forearm use can be re-moved and reattached by using dual stock-mount-ed sling swivels. This permits pop-ular subma-chine gun carry of the midrange carbine: looped round the neck, the carbine can be used from either shoulder. Looping it around the neck and one shoulder ensures secure carry and weapon retention. By using this method of carry the shooter can safely drop the carbine in place and switch to a handgun if required. However, you must use cau-tion when attaching a weapon to your body by a sling. If the sling is unre-leasable, especially when it is worn around the neck, an unexpected gun-grab situation can result in injury.

Slings can be beneficial in the right situations. At other times, they can be a snagging nuisance. Your

The D.L. sling system can add substantial stability to shooting positions when hard support is not available.

Over-the-neck, subma-chine-gun-style carry pro-vides support and ambi-dextrous operation.

A carbine or full-sized firearm should be chosen based on individual requirements.

sling-equipped carbine should also feature quick detachments or a sling-hanger system to keep the sling taut and out of the way when not in use. Do not let the sling "hang and sway" when shooting offhand; it will cause rifle disturbance. To see just how much this can affect your sight picture, aim at a target while standing off-hand and have your partner start the sling swaying, as if by the wind. It has a noticeable effect on your stability. This is especially true if you have a data bag hanging on your sling.

A sensible contour match-grade barrel added to the custom carbine package will allow sub-MOA accuracy, while keeping the weight and overall length down to a fast-handling compact size. Barrel fluting can also be added to further reduce overall weight, maintain rigidity, and improve barrel cooling.

The stock of the custom carbine can be suited to the individual shooter's body dimensions. A full-sized stock can have butt spacers added if extra length is required for the long-limbed shooter. The collapsible stock is often cursed for being too short for the adult U.S. male shooter, but many of the same people find the collapsible stock quite functional when they are equipped with a thick tactical vest. To determine the best stock length, you must try different stocks while dressed as you would be on a call-out. Avoid any unnecessary clutter in your stock's shoulder-mounting area. Items such as badges, radio

The accuracy of the match-barreled carbine, combined with its handiness, makes it an excellent midrange choice. The full-size custom ARs also perform well in the accuracy department.

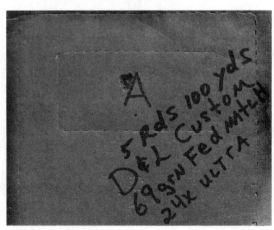

microphones, pens, and notebooks interfere with stock shouldering. In situations that require you to have a badge in place for identification purposes, a sewn-on cloth badge is preferable to a metal one. The collapsible stock is only a slight advantage in vehicular-transport situations. The field-cleaning gear compartment of the full stock makes it the more practical unit.

The AR-15-style rifle has become popular among serious shooters in recent years. Demands for increased AR performance have led to the development of substantially improved trigger systems.

Triggering systems for the AR-style rifle are currently available in single-stage, two-stage, and third-generation set triggers. These

A top-quality midrange carbine is well suited to the patrol officer, tactical marksman, and action shooter's needs.

The fast-handling carbine facilitates instantaneous responses and action shooting.

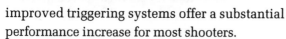

improved triggering systems offer a substantial performance increase for most shooters.

The trigger setting feature is available for the AR-style as well as the bolt-action rifles. The trigger-setting feature is normally selective, meaning that it is the operator's option whether to "set" the trigger for a light release. Setting your trigger mechanism to release with an extremely light trigger pull at certain times and stiffer pulls at other times hampers consistency in training and operation. Consistency leads to familiarity, which translates into performance. If you complicate your situation with unnecessary decisions—to set or not to set—make sure you are well aware of how to safely unset the trigger when a shot is called off at the last second. The set systems work well for target or varmint work, but I do not use or recommend them for tactical use.

Action rifle competition often simulates situations and ranges in which a law enforcement

A custom, heavy-barreled AR-15 with muzzle brake. This system recoils so lightly that a shooter can easily watch his own rounds hit on target.

The high sightline of the standard-scope-mounted AR-15 results in low hits at point-blank range unless substantial compensation is made. This can be disastrous in fast action. The properly low-scoped and zeroed AR-15 places the shots with less difficulty.

officer could expect to use a midrange rifle. Experimentation, development, and refinement in this style of competition, as well as live tactical situations, have contributed to the success of the low-scoped AR-15-style rifle. Many professional shooters agree that when the custom low-scoped AR-15 is used within its suited parameters, it is the best selection available.

NUMBER OF RIFLES REQUIRED

Beyond common midrange rifle distances, the precision rifle becomes the right tool for the job. I'm a believer in keeping things as simple as possible, provided the simple solution achieves acceptable performance. You may consider using just one rifle for distances from point-blank to extended range. This would allow training with one rifle, one load, one sight—and only the requirement of being familiar with one trajectory, wind drift, and trigger pull.

In theory, it sounds like the best way to be familiar with your equipment, just as the old saying of "beware the one-gun man" suggests. However, closer evaluation of the requirements of shooting from close to long range may change your mind slightly. The one-familiar-rifle rule may require expansion into a two-rifle concept to cover all the situations a tactical marksman must be prepared to encounter. Even the two-rifle concept does not include specialized assignments, such as extreme-range shooting or heavy-barrier penetration. Special operations military units that have personnel training full time commonly issue four to five rifles, plus night vision devices, to their snipers. This may include the M16, M14, a .308 Winchester bolt-action rifle, .300 Winchester Magnum (WM), and .50 Browning Machine Gun (BMG) bolt gun. The rifle best suited for the mission at hand is then selected. Keep in mind that these operators have the luxury of training full time. Familiarity with all issued weapons is a must.

The two-rifle principle should meet the requirements faced by a nonmilitary tactical marksman in most situations; it is effective in standard operations from close to extended ranges on unarmored targets. But remember that you'll have to double the training time necessary to become familiar with one rifle.

A marksman required to cover a wide gamut of distances but preferring a single rifle should probably choose a semiauto rifle chambered for a full-powered cartridge. A com-

The professional-grade MR-30 and 5.56mm carbine make a superior two-gun system. The MR-30PG rifle is also available in a takedown version.

monly available caliber suitable as a compromise between short and long distances is the .308 Winchester. A full-sized semiautomatic battle rifle would allow a shooter to cover the various distances but would probably not achieve best performance at any distance. At close to medium distances, in close quarters, the cumbersome battle rifle is awkward, and recoil slows down accurate multiple-target fire for most shooters. At extended ranges, the less-than-precise mechanical semiauto accuracy, .308 Winchester trajectory and field-grade trigger pull impede proper shot placement. An accurized .308 Winchester semiauto, such as the HK PSG-1, is accurate and has good trigger pull, but true fast

A custom .50-caliber rifle on a McMillan action. Note the effective clamshell muzzle brake. Lynn McMurdo won first place in the 1995 Nationals with this rifle.

Barrett Model 82A1 .50-caliber semiauto rifle.

Agencies that choose to put heavy-caliber counter-sniper equipment "on call" must also consider how to get everything "on scene." The M82A1 soft mount works well.

A SAR 4800 semiauto 7.62mm and an HK 91 7.62mm semiauto.

handling at close range is seriously handicapped because of the rifle's size and weight. At extended ranges, it still has .308 ballistics.

If you decide to go with just one rifle, it should have just one scope attached to it. Close to medium distances and fast action are best served with a lower magnification scope; whereas long-range target identification and precise shot placement are better suited to a higher magnification scope. The logical solution is a variable scope from low to high magnification. A large variable scope not only adds to the rifle's weight and awkwardness at close range, it also adds variable scope tolerances (provided it is not a first focal plane reticle) at longer ranges, where precision is most needed.

Considering the drawbacks of the one-rifle idea, it is necessary to amend the "keep it simple" principle to "keep it as simple as possible while still meeting performance standards." This means that your light carbine must be backed up by an extended-range precision rifle to be most effective at all the practical distances you may be expected to cover.

Field rifle accuracy considered precise by today's standards is that capable of

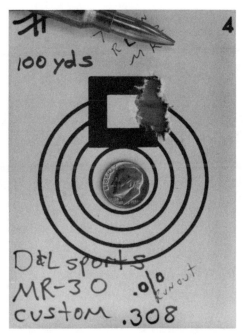

Precision equipment and top-quality training lead to top performance even under rugged field conditions.

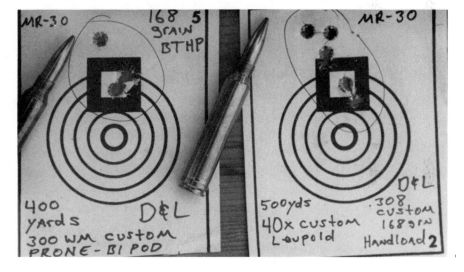

repeatable sub-MOA performance in harsh conditions. In most cases, to achieve this accuracy you need a finely tuned bolt-action rifle. Uncle Joe's deer rifle or mass-produced bolt guns with black stocks marketed as "sniper rifles" just won't cut it. Departmental "bean counters" may try to press marginally accurate rifles into service based on cost alone. This violates the accepted standard in precision riflery and fails to take into account human variables. A shooter equipped with a system capable of 1/4 MOA mechanical accuracy knows that accuracy achieved in excess of 1/4 MOA is caused by environmental conditions or human error.

The data developed with an inaccurate rifle is also questionable. For example, you may want to develop data on how temperature affects POI. With a 1/4 MOA rifle you should be able to watch any shot group movement and be confident that it is the result of temperature differences. With a 2 MOA rifle, the shot group is not consistently tight enough to determine the effect of temperature alone.

Rifle inaccuracy and additional real-world adverse conditions add up to unacceptable performance. The quality and accuracy of your precision rifle system may mean life or death for a hostage. Budgetary concerns should not be your top priority; reliable, accurate performance must be.

A precision rifle properly built around a top-quality, accurized bolt action provides consistent accuracy unattainable with less rigid action lockups. For top performance,

the action must be true and square to allow proper barrel alignment with the action.

Overall action trueness and alignment with a properly fitted and chambered match-grade barrel provide correct, consistent chambering and precise bullet alignment with the bore. Without this precision-fit, you cannot consistently attain top accuracy.

The action should feature a fast lock time to minimize POI disturbance

A D & L MR-30 precision rifle with camouflaged adjustable fiberglass stock. The Remington Model 700 action is hard chrome; the fluted super-match barrel is stainless steel, and the scope is a Leupold Ultra. The entire unit should be camouflaged before serious field use, thus making a camouflaged veil on the rifle less critical.

resulting from rifle movement after the trigger break. (Lock time is the amount of time from sear release to cartridge ignition.) A quick lock time minimizes the amount of time between the trigger break and cartridge ignition. Less time to ignite means less time available for the rifle to move off target after the sear is released.

Even with quick lock times, measured in thousandths of a second and using supersonic projectiles, you should practice proper follow-through to prevent rifle disturbance while the cartridge is being ignited and the bullet is traveling through the barrel. Briefly hold your sight picture on target following trigger break. Do not break the trigger and then collapse your hold, or shot dispersion will occur.

COMPONENTS

Stock

The first item to consider is the stock. It must hold the action rigidly and consistently, neither flexing under recoil nor warping with changes in moisture, temperature, and humidity. Stock warpage affects how the action is held, and pressures on the barrel can rob you of accuracy. Wood stocks are not suitable for the tactical marksman operating in a variety of environments. High-tech synthetic or fiberglass stocks, such as the top-quality McMillan and HS Precision, should be considered mandatory on the tactical marksman's rifle. Having a professional bed, the barreled action to a fiberglass stock enhances consistency under a wide range of conditions.

The stock must fit the shooter to obtain optimal performance, giving proper cheek weld, scope eye relief, and hand grip. This can be most effectively accomplished by using a stock adjustable for both length of pull and cheekpiece height. An adjustable buttplate that allows the recoil pad to move up or down permits the shooter to fine-tune the butt-shoulder positioning for his most frequently used position. Once the stock is adjusted for the operator, I recommend using it as is, without repeatedly adjusting it for minor position changes. Always strive for consistency, using the same rifle setup each time.

Stocks can be obtained with full-length forearm rails, with or without handstops. These rails are normally used in conjunction with sling support. Formal "loop slinging" has proven impractical in tactical encounters because of the time it takes to assume the formal loop and the length of time for which most shooters can hold a rifle in this manner. I have found that a series of securely anchored sling studs mounted on the underside of the stock is most useful. Securely anchored means using studs with large backers inside the barrel channel, not simply screwing the studs into the stock. A series of three studs on the underside of the forearm permits attachment of a bipod to the front stud, and a quick-detachable D.L. sling to the rearmost two studs. The D.L. is quick to assume and adds substantial stability when solid support is unavailable. A fourth stud can be placed in the underside of the butt for standard sling carry or hasty sling use. The studded stock would not be suitable for benchresters shooting free-recoil on talcum bags, but the tactical marksman should be more concerned with field practicality.

Trigger Group

The action should be capable of accepting a high-quality trigger group. A clean, precise trigger is a must for precision shooting. This does not mean an excessively lightweight trigger pull or an unsafe trigger-sear engagement. I do not recommend reworking factory trigger groups, and neither do most factories. If you use a stock trigger, use the factory-adjusted pull weight. If you don't, the factory will obviously claim that your modification of its trigger created any mishap that may have occurred. Many tactical rifle custom shops don't take this into consideration and continue to modify factory trigger groups. I use only match-quality trigger groups that are certified for law enforcement duty use. Precision-made trigger groups are a much better choice because they come in specific pull-weight ranges. Yes, top-quality costs more, but a reliable trigger needs to be one of your highest priorities. No matter which route you decide to go, you must thoroughly test the reliability of your trigger group under expected field conditions before duty use. This may include extreme cold, heat, sand, and, of course, rapid bolt operation. Any unintentional firings during rapid bolt closure indicate that the rifle is not suitable for duty use until the source of the problem is pinpointed and corrected.

Precision-trigger groups are manufactured in trigger-pull-weight ranges well suited to the tactical marksman. These trigger groups are manufactured to safely and reliably operate in their specified pull ranges. Do not cut corners in this critical area of safety and performance.

The best trigger-pull weight depends on the experience of the marksman. Extremely light target triggers are not recommended for use in live situations; 2-ounce benchrest triggers should not even be considered for tactical use. Less experienced shooters should stay in the 4-pound range. Unintentional discharges are unacceptable; to be safe, don't use a trigger beyond your experience level.

Experienced marksmen may settle on lower trigger-pull weights that fill their individual requirements. Experienced shooters develop a trigger finger that operates independently of the grip of the rest of the hand. This "experienced finger" is capable of superb trigger control.

Trigger adjustment work is a job for the experienced armorer. Do not attempt to lighten a factory-adjusted trigger. Reducing sear engagement, spring pressure, and pull weight beyond what a standard factory trigger is rated for is unwise, to say the least. A precision trigger group designed to be reliable at the lighter weights is the best way to achieve an excellent, reliable pull. Even trigger groups specifically designed to be adjusted should still only be adjusted by an experienced armorer. These adjustments should be made with reliability as a top priority and "set" in place to avoid future "walking" of the adjustments. Ask the armorer doing the final trigger work about proper maintenance procedures for the trigger group.

An all-stainless-steel or plated trigger group requires minimal maintenance in the field. A dirty or dusty trigger group is best cleaned by flushing it with lighter fluid. Do not lubricate it because this will attract dirt. More substantial contamination should be attended to by an armorer, which also gives him an opportunity to retest engagements.

Any trigger work should be followed by thorough range testing before the rifle is put back into service.

Bolt Actions

High-quality custom actions are available from Hall, McMillan, Kelby, Shilen, and Hart. These actions are built with precision accuracy as a primary goal, and their price reflects it. They are common on the benchrest circuit.

Many of the custom and sleeved actions are single shots only. This allows for more rigidity and more bedding surface. The tactical marksman should acquire a repeating action to facilitate quick, follow-up shots. One shot-one hit is always the precision marksman's goal, but Murphy's Law and multiple targets must be planned for.

As have other precision shooters, I have found the Remington Model 700 action an excellent starting point for creating a precision rifle. This action will accept cartridges well suited to tactical unit selection and is available with a magazine. The magazine-cut action is less rigid than a single shot, but backup rounds could be critical in a tactical situation. With accurizing work, the Remington magazine-fed Model 700 action provides precision accuracy.

The Model 700 Remington action is similar to the Model 1911 auto pistol in that both make excellent bases for building a custom firearm; however, both have several areas that need special attention before they meet performance standards. These areas of the 700 include squaring and truing the action and bolt face, lapping the bolt lugs, smoothing the ways, tuning the extractor, installing heavy steel trigger guard/floorplate assembly and bolt stop, reinforcing the scope base mounting, installing a heavier lug, and reinforcing the bolt handle. As of this date, no other custom action or rifle has been able to surpass the custom 700 in overall terms of accuracy, reliability, and ruggedness.

The 700 action is available in both right- and left-handed versions. The right-handed action is still the recommended choice for the left-handed shooter. The right-handed action can be bedded into a left-hand grip or ambidextrous stock to allow the southpaw shooter to fire from the left shoulder. When the firearm is artificially supported, as with a bipod, the southpaw can use his right hand to operate the bolt, while maintaining a firing grip on the stock. This allows fast follow-up shots. Some people speculate that this may have been the fast-firing technique used by left-handed Lee Harvey Oswald when he allegedly assassinated President John Kennedy.

Extra-long-range specialty rifles capable of handling extralarge cartridges are normally built on custom bolt actions resembling upscaled 700s but frequently weighing three times as much. This is a tribute to the Model 700's design. The long-range accuracy of the specialty rifles in the hands of a professional is excellent. Sub-5-inch groups at 1,200 yards have been recorded.

Your precision rifle should be rugged, with safe, reliable, repeatable accuracy as the top priority. The components on a modern precision rifle have developed over many years of research and testing to ensure safe, reliable accuracy. The modern precision rifle is a giant step above the general-production rifle, and it will continue to develop in the future for one main reason: it will be called upon for use in an arena where failure could very easily mean death to an innocent person. Marksmen who do not demand the best equipment and administrators who do not procure it are not doing their best to ensure successful missions.

When selecting your precision rifle you should be aware of what to look for.

Barrel

The precision rifle's barrel must be of the best quality available if top performance is expected. Production-line budget barrels are not acceptable. The barrel must consistently send bullets out on the same line. Barrel-damaged bullets lead to inaccuracy, so the barrel must be uniform. The barrel must have a straight bore with an excellent finish to deliver undamaged bullets into flight.

The two most popular methods of rifling benchrest-quality barrels are "cut" and "button." The cut process is accomplished by cutting individual grooves in succession, whereas the button method involves pulling a steel or carbide slug through the lubricated barrel. The slug transfers its shape of lands and grooves to the barrel's interior.

Both methods produce excellent results when done properly, so on-target accuracy should determine which you choose.

Top-quality stainless steel should be your choice of barrel material. It remains accurate longer than other steels and is more resistant to the elements.

The steel must be "clean." Steel containing foreign contamination suffers from pitting as the foreign material burns out during firing. The pits gather fouling and jacket material, decreasing accuracy. Cleaner steel results in fewer pits and prolonged accuracy. The best way to ensure that your rifle has a "clean" barrel is to use the finest barrels from the most reputable manufacturers.

The finest grade barrels receive special attention all the way through the manufacturing process. The best grades of barrels are finish-lapped for a smooth bore and reduced fouling.

It is common for a top-grade barrel to have only .0001- to .0002-inch variance on the groove diameter for the entire length of the barrel. True premium-grade stainless barrels are so precise and accurate that aftermarket accuracy-enhancement treatments are not needed. Barrels with these exacting dimensions, along with precision chambering and crowning, when properly combined with an accurized action, deliver mechanical accuracy. Combine precision ammunition and quality optics and mounts, add a well-trained marksman, and you have on-target performance.

The twist rate of the barrel must be properly chosen for the bullet you intend to

Specialized operations may require high-performance equipment. The .50 BMG can deliver high performance in experienced hands. If you expect to use specialized equipment on a call-out, you must train with it diligently and develop all the necessary field-expedient data. New developments in the .50 BMG area can be obtained from the .50-Cal BMG Shooters Association in St. Louis, Missouri, or from some specialized military units.

shoot. It is best to know what bullet you will be shooting before you order your barrel twist. In .30-caliber barrels, 1 turn in 12 inches works well with bullets in the medium-weight range. Heavier bullets are better suited to the 1 turn in 10 inches. Extralight or heavy bullets require additional evaluation of twist rate for best performance. Barrel length and diameter should also be a consideration in your rifle selection. A shorter, lighter barrel (e.g., 22 to 24 inches and .900 inch at the muzzle) will work well on rifles intended for faster handling. This is a fairly common dimension for 7.62mm bolt-action rifles. Magnum rifles with a large charge of slow-burning powder can take advantage of added barrel length to generate higher velocities. Barrels of 26 to 29 inches are common in magnums intended for enhanced ballistic performance and longer ranges. A stouter barrel means a stiffer barrel that supplements accuracy.

Handling and portability factors come into play here. The exact length and weight considered balanced and portable vary from person to person. Some shooters prefer a

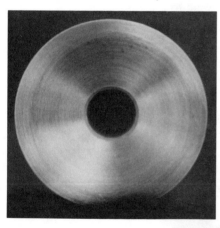

full-sized rifle while others favor the transport ease of the MR-30PGTDR (.30-caliber, professional-grade, takedown marksman's rifle). Barrel length can vary from 16.5 to 36 inches. Total bull barrel rifle weight usually ranges from 10 to 20 pounds; this weight is heavily influenced by the barrel contour you select. You should have enough total weight to dampen recoil and add consistency, but not too much to be portable. The big, extended-range rifles in the .30-378, .338-378, and .50-caliber range can easily weigh 20 to 50 pounds, complete with 34-to-36-inch length, 1.500-inch-diameter barrel. Always keep in mind that you have to hump whatever rifle you select—and that's along with a host of other gear.

Barrel fluting has become a popular option because it maintains rigidity and

A high-quality stock and muzzle brake do much to keep recoil comfortable. Barrel fluting reduces weight, maintains rigidity, and improves cooling.

reduces weight. Fluting also creates a larger surface area to reduce cooling time. This is important since heat is a major factor in barrel wear. If a barrel is too hot to touch comfortably, avoid shooting until it's cooled and cleaned.

The barrel should feature a precision-turned crown for consistent

The precision rifle's muzzle should be properly crowned to ensure proper bullet release. A recessed crown protects the rifling from damage. A muzzle brake protects the muzzle and reduces felt recoil. A muzzle brake also increases the need for a ground cloth.

bullet release. The crown should be recessed or covered by a muzzle brake for rifling protection. A ground cloth is especially important if you choose a muzzle brake, because the blast can kick up loose ground material and move surrounding vegetation. This can have several adverse effects, including disclosing your position, obstructing the target, and propelling foreign matter into your eyes.

When you acquire a new precision rifle with a top-grade match barrel, you should follow the barrel break-in procedure listed in the maintenance section of this book for the best accuracy and longevity.

Even the best quality and most meticulously maintained barrels will not deliver top accuracy forever. If you are considering a used rifle, barrel wear should be an important consideration. Accurate, honest records of the number of rounds fired and maintenance may be hard to come by. A borescope inspection as well as on-target performance is OK, but the best advice is to start off with a new rifle and maintain it properly for greatest barrel life.

A milder cartridge, such as the .308 Winchester, gives accurate barrel life longer than the hotter .300 WM, and the hot .30-378 provides even less life than the .300 WM. You have to pay for the higher ballistic performance somewhere, and accurate barrel life is one of these areas. Proper maintenance increases barrel life, but to maintain optimal accuracy you should budget for barrel replacement every 2,500 to 5,000 rounds on the .308 Winchester; 1,000 rounds on the .300 WM; and 500 to 800 rounds on the hot wildcats. Beyond these limits, precision and ballistic performance suffer noticeably; higher performance always takes a toll on the barrel's life and on the shooter's pocketbook. Maintaining high performance is normally an accepted and expected cost of being a precision marksman, and performance is what separates the professional from the plinker.

Correct selection of your extended-range rifle caliber depends on your requirements. If your situation indicates that shooting beyond 500 yards is unrealistic, such as in a confined urban environment, a precision-built .308 Winchester rifle will probably suit your needs.

Ammunition

Factory match-grade ammunition loaded with accurate boat-tail hollow point (BTHP) bullets is available for the .308 Winchester. It is also commonly accepted as a police countersniper cartridge. Federal Cartridge Company has also introduced a .308 tactical load. The bonded core bullet used in this load is more suited to glass penetration without fragmentation than is the Sierra Match King bullet. It is not as accurate but maintains a similar trajectory pattern as the Match bullet at ranges less than 200 yards. Thorough testing and evaluation are required before putting multiple loads on call.

A precision bolt-action .308 Winchester rifle is certainly capable of accuracy far beyond 500 yards, but when wind and distance are unknown and have to be estimated, and a first-round hit is required, other calibers provide a larger margin of error.

Comparing the performance charts of factory .308 match ammunition to a cartridge with better long-range performance, such as the .300 WM, may lead a performance-oriented officer to look further than the accepted standard. This is especially true when he is expected to handle the longer ranges found at airports or in rural areas. Extended-range cartridges are in constant development. Look for new long-range products for Magnum performance from beltless factory ammunition in the future.

When selecting a cartridge, you must consider more than just accuracy. The BTHP bullet used in Match loadings is designed for match accuracy and does an excellent job of achieving it. Personal tests on glass penetration and torso game shots indicate that the manufacturer's statement that the bullet was designed for neither hunting or nonfragmenting penetration is correct. Serious deflection and fragmentation on glass and minimal terminal performance on torso-shot game have been the norm. These were 168-grain BTHPs traveling at a muzzle velocity of 2,650 feet per second (FPS). Close-range urban shooting situations may allow for exact bullet placement into the no-reflex zone and suspect neutralization, but longer ranges may require torso-aimed shots to ensure hits. Torso hits, and possibly shots fired through glass or other barriers, may require better bullet performance. An experienced tactical unit, aware of the weak performance areas of the commonly accepted Match bullet, may incur liability by not selecting a bullet that performs the required task better or more safely. An anticipated failure resulting in harm to an innocent person should be of more concern than cost. Marksmen should test and document the performance of their bullets so that they know their bullets' capabilities. The quest for performance may never be over, but we must keep striving for the best results possible. One area that deserves more attention is that of accurate, high-performance bullets (see Chapter 5 on ammunition for more information).

Tactical marksman must evaluate their distance requirements thoroughly; even urban environments can present the tactical marksman with substantial distances. A marksman given a countersniper mission may find that his target has selected a distant, more advantageous position. Marksmen operating in areas where people are more shooting oriented may face individuals with more firearms "reach" than the officers had prepared for. Rural communities often have a lot of people who own long guns and who have developed their shooting skills over a lifetime of hunting and shooting. The plains areas of the United States are host to a multitude of people who commonly shoot 3-by-6-inch varmints at 300 to 500 yards and beyond. Serious shooters receive awards for scoring hits from 500 to 2,500 yards, and some shooters compete to hit a chicken egg with one shot at 500 yards. The huge majority of these shooters are law-abiding, but as all tactical officers know, many people can react adversely to personal problems. A highly skilled shooter reacting poorly to a problem can make the situation more difficult for a tactical unit.

A Canadian tactical officer stated that there are more incidents with long guns than handguns; the limited availability of handguns in Canada forces hostiles there to arm themselves with more powerful weapons, thereby extending their range capabilities. Tactical officers dealing with experienced rifle shooters holed up in remote locations or atop tall buildings may also face longer range encounters. A survivalist or radical may put detailed planning into the defensibility of his retreat and eliminate close-range accessibility.

Urban officers may face a long-range encounter as well. A countersniper instructor recently related an incident in which a deranged man armed with a rifle took over a public gathering spot in a large city and commanded a huge field of fire: a tactical extended-range marksman was reportedly required to resolve the incident at slightly more than 500 yards. The 1993 Branch Davidian standoff in Waco, Texas, demonstrated that tactical marksmen may even be exposed to riflemen equipped with .50 BMG rifles.

Proper training and equipment are essential to defeat well-equipped adversaries. Realistic evaluation of the possible extended-distance requirements a marksman may face in his call-out area is necessary to determine which precision rifle and caliber best suit his needs. If the expected range exceeds 500 yards, numerous calibers offer a better trajectory than the .308 Winchester. There is more to consider than trajectory when selecting a cartridge for tactical use, even though it is an important consideration when shooting at estimated ranges. It should be evaluated along with accuracy, wind deflection, recoil, Match ammo availability, bullet selection, and performance, as well as overall field practicality and portability.

Varmint calibers offer high velocity, flat trajectory and excellent accuracy, but suffer in extended-range ballistic performance, as well as inconsistent bullet penetration and fragmentation.

Heavier cartridges, such as the .338 Lapua Magnum, .30-378, .338-378, .30-416, and .50-caliber BMG, give excellent long-range performance, but not without increased recoil and difficult portability. These cartridges, fired out of accurized rifles, are capable of sub-1/2 MOA at 1,000 yards and beyond. These cartridges may fill an important role in some specialized military or tactical operations but are normally too much rifle to be practical for average tactical operations. Also keep in mind that a pet wildcat cartridge requires detailed and specialized ammunition preparation. These endeavors consume a lot of time, require substantial expertise, and will probably come under close post-shooting scrutiny.

A cartridge that outperforms the typical .308 Winchester Match cartridge is the .300 WM. The .300 WM maintains the .30-caliber bullet selection and improved ballistics without requiring an excessively large rifle. The .300 WM is not without its drawbacks: the bull-barreled .300 WM rifle is a step up in size and weight from the .308 Winchester, has more felt recoil, and suffers from barrel-throat erosion more quickly. You must take these factors, along with ammunition for the .300 WM, into consideration before selecting this cartridge. (Shooters who are recoil sensitive may develop flinching or other poor shooting habits if the .300 WM is not properly set up to suit them.) If you do select the .300 WM, cure this problem before it occurs by setting the rifle up to recoil as lightly as possible. There is no need, and no gain, in shooting a rifle with more recoil just to prove you can take it. Down-range, on-target performance is the objective, not a macho image. High-ballistic performance may require a higher recoiling cartridge, but proper shooting technique, stock design, recoil pad, muzzle brake, and shooting garments help keep the recoil felt by the shooter to a minimum.

Shooters willing to make the commitment to handling the .300 WM properly will benefit from this higher performance cartridge at longer ranges. Superior trajectory, wind resistance, and energy all favor the .300 WM.

What this means in field performance is that the .300 WM is more forgiving when it comes to distance and wind estimations. This means higher hit probability at extended ranges. For example, a shooter fires a .308 Winchester Match load with a 168-grain bullet at 2,500 fps at a 600-yard target but incorrectly estimates the range by 100 yards (an easy mistake by an inexperienced range estimator). The bullet would be off the mark by approximately 40 inches. The same mistake made by the .300 WM shooter would result in a bullet only 22 inches off the mark.

At 1,000 yards the .308 Winchester zeroed at 100 yards will drop an additional 406 inches, the .300 only 214 inches—almost a 50-percent better hit probability.

The wind-drift advantage also goes to the .300 WM over the .308 Winchester at all ranges. At 1,000 yards the .308 Winchester drifts 88 inches in a 10-mph, 90-degree crosswind, and the .300 WM only 58 inches in the same wind.

The properly loaded .300 WM has a substantial flight advantage over the .308 Winchester 168-grain factory-match load, and the higher velocity of the .300 WM appears to dramatically increase terminal ballistics on torso-shot game.

The current philosophy among tactical marksmen is that they can use proper fieldcraft to get well within 500 yards of a target, normally under 100 yards, thus allowing them to use the established, accurate, and reliable .308 Winchester cartridge effectively. Shooting the .308 permits use of factory-loaded, accurate match and tactical ammunition. If shooting beyond 500 yards is realistic in your environment, cartridges in .300WM, .338 Lapua, and .50-caliber BMG should be evaluated.

RIFLE SELECTION SUMMARY

Evaluate your needs and research what is available, keeping in mind that the right tool for the job is the one that gives the best performance.

In my opinion, the tactical marksman required to cover close to long distances should use two rifles: a light-caliber, semiauto carbine capable of close to medium ranges, quick yet precise fire, and a precision bolt-action rifle capable of accurate bullet placement out to the maximum ranges an officer may encounter. A .30-caliber bolt rifle allows the shooter to choose from a variety of quality bullets to achieve accuracy, penetration, and terminal ballistics.

In my experience, this two-rifle arrangement covers the majority of general tactical call-outs. Of course, more specialized missions may require more specialized equipment.

Reliable, repeatable accuracy is a must for rifles selected for use on tactical missions. Do not make selections based on budget over performance, because equipment may be the deciding factor between success and failure. Don't be a gadgeteer; make your selections based on realistic field performance.

Optics and Support Equipment

WHEN YOU CHOOSE OPTICS AND SUPPORT EQUIPMENT, REALISTIC EVALUATION OF YOUR needs and requirements is in order. If you decide to go with two rifles, you have to choose the optics best suited to the role each will fulfill.

Although some shooters argue in favor of iron sights, at least for the midrange rifle, citing more ruggedness and less chance of zero loss, I prefer scope sights for two reasons. First, the rifles selected are intended for a professional marksman, who takes care of and maintains his equipment. Second, ruggedness and reliability are not forfeited with today's top-quality scopes and mountings—and scope sights offer several sighting advantages over iron sights. These advantages are obviously being taken seriously by designers of futuristic military rifles because many of the designers are incorporating scope sights.

Rifle scope selection should be based on quality, not price. Purchasing the weekly special at a local discount store probably is not the most direct route to quality optics. Purchase correctly the first time, especially if you are responsible for government purchases. Whether you're buying optics or any other expensive items, having to confess to administrators that what you purchased failed to meet the needs of your team will not make you popular. Repeated examples of your inadequate research on equipment recommendations will lead to your loss of credibility.

I have had good results with rifle scopes from Leupold, Zeiss, Schmidt Bender, Oakshore, and Kahles. Gale McMillan has formed a scope company and introduced

Leupold 3.5-10x with 50mm objective.

39

a rifle scope in the 2.5-10x range with a 30mm tube that looks very promising. Unertl also offers high-quality internally adjustable scopes, but their availability is limited. Unertl's externally adjustable scopes are popular with long-range benchrest shooters because of their superior optics and generous elevation adjustment. But for field use, I prefer the more compact and less cluttered style of the internally adjusted scopes over the larger externally adjustable scopes.

The midrange rifle is designed for use at point-blank-to-medium distances. The scope chosen to top this rifle should suit the primary ranges that you expect to encounter. A point-blank zero is best for the fast-action carbine. The carbine-scope combination should also be able to withstand rigorous use in all environments. There is little need for the obtrusive target knobs on the carbine scope; they only serve as protrusions for damage and snagging.

The scopes for the carbine and the precision rifle should both feature positive "click" adjustments rather than friction adjustments. These click adjustments should be no larger than 1/4 MOA or 1/4 inch.

A variable scope works best for the distances the midrange carbine is expected to cover. The ideal choice is a scope sight capable of low magnification for a wide field of view and quick target acquisition during close-range action. The same scope should be capable of enough magnification for positive target identification and shot placement at medium ranges.

Several quality scopes are available in these suitable power ranges: 1.5–5x, 1.5–6x, 1.75–6x, 2–7x, 3–9x, 2.5–10x, 3.5–10x, and 3x12.

Any variable-magnification scope, even from a reputable manufacturer, must be thoroughly tested for impact changes at different power settings. The simplest procedure is to fire the best 10-round, slow-fire group possible with the scope set at a single power setting. Fire another 10-round, slow-fire group, changing the power setting between each shot. The magnification changes should be made as they would be under realistic field conditions: not smooth, complete power ring rotations, but alternating short and long, jerky, and incomplete rotations. The second slow-fire group should not be noticeably larger than the first. If it is, get a new scope for duty use.

Another way to check scope zero variations during power and adjustable objective changes is by using a collimator. Simply watch the reticle on the collimator's grid while making changes in the settings. Any noticeable reticle movement during adjustments renders the scope unsuitable for duty use.

Some custom variable-scope manufacturers place the reticle in the first focal plane to eliminate any impact shift when changing powers. This also causes the reticle size to go up and down with the magnification. This seems to be distracting to some shooters because on high magnification the reticle appears quite thick, and a thick reticle can obscure a distant target. On the positive side, this type of reticle placement keeps reticle-ranging procedures constant at any magnification and shows up well in low light.

I prefer to keep the medium-range carbine scope as simple as performance standards allow. This means that the adjustable-scope objective is undesirable. Provided that you use the proper magnification for the distance encountered, the scope is clear throughout the entire range of distances expected to be encountered, and parallax error at close to medium range is minimal. The adjustable objective (AO) is just another feature to be out of adjustment on a hasty response.

Should your carbine's scope feature an AO, check it by going through the same 10-shot grouping or collimator procedure as you did with the magnification. In tactical environments, nothing should be left to chance.

The variable-magnification scope, with or without AO, should be stored at its lowest magnification and AO settings so that it will be ready for any close-range action. (Longer range situations should allow time to make any needed scope adjustments.) The carbine should be kept in an "on-duty" status, with a slightly short-loaded magazine in place, chamber empty, safety off, stock extended, hammer down, and sling secured, thus permitting a prompt response to close-range action by simply chambering a round. The rifle's springs are not fully compressed to avoid spring set, and the secured sling is not snag prone. A rifle stored in this condition for extended periods should have the magazine emptied and replaced at least every 30 days. New magazine springs should be installed at least every six months if magazines are kept on an on-duty status. Weakening springs can result in reliability problems.

As of this writing, I have had good results from midrange carbines fitted with variable-magnification scopes in the 1.5–12x range. Several scopes from the previously listed manufacturers fall into these ranges. A top-quality scope mounted to a midrange carbine using a low rail mount and multiple rings is very rugged. The multiple-ring mount provides both rigidity and scope-tube protection should the rifle be dropped on the scope. Rubber-armored scope "bells" will also help to absorb any impact they may receive, as well as deadening any resulting noise. Nonfactory rubber-armored scopes may not be aesthetically pleasing, but they are field practical.

Swarovski/Barrett 10x .50-caliber rifle scope with Barrett 30mm steel rings and Barrett Dovetail Mount for Kigre Night Vision.

The actual power range a shooter selects depends on his shooting experience with a scope and his willingness to train with his selection. The higher the scope's magnification, the smaller the field of view (FOV). Experienced scope shooters normally have little problem indexing on a point-blank target on 3.5x. Novice shooters may be more comfortable with a 1.5x magnification on the low end of the variable-power scale. A midrange carbine scope with a substantial "top end" magnification provides the best target identification and shot placement at midranges. A midrange carbine scope in the ranges of 1.5–6x, 2–7x, 2.5–10x, 3–9x, 3.5–10x, or 3–12x should meet the requirements of most shooters.

The carbine scope should be well suited to use in low-light conditions. A top-quality objective lens in the 32–50mm range gives good light transmission without the obtrusiveness of a 56mm scope mounted on a carbine. Scopes with an objective lens smaller than 32mm should be avoided for low-light shooting.

A carbine scope with a selective reticle light is also desirable. The reticle should be adjustable from very dim to very bright. The dim setting works well for shooting under existing low-light conditions on a dark target. Too much reticle light will wash out the target and disturb night vision in your shooting eye. A bright contrasting reticle works well when illuminating a target with a high-intensity spotlight, hence the need for dim to bright adjustability.

Several lighted reticle scopes have "floating" aiming points, which must be thoroughly evaluated for parallax problems before selection or use. To do this, secure the scope rigidly in place and then move your eye around behind the eyepiece. If the aiming point or reticle "swims" or appears to move, in relation to the targets, it is not suitable for duty use.

The requirements for a scope for the long-range precision rifle are greater than those for the midrange carbine.

If you don't agree with the two-rifle concept and are going to make a single rifle fit any situation, you must select your scope accordingly. You might consider a variable-magnification scope to cover all distances you expect to encounter.

Many urban officers have chosen or have been issued the 3.5–10x Leupold for their precision rifles. The lower magnification works fine at the statistically indicated closer ranges, but the maximum 10x at longer ranges limits target identification and shot placement. If you choose magnification in this range, be sure it meets your requirements.

Leupold and other companies offer variable scopes in the 6.5–20x range. Leupold's scope has performed well for both target identification and shot placement at extended ranges, but the low-end magnification of 6.5x makes it difficult for some shooters to use at very close ranges. The limited elevation adjustments of these standard target/varmint scopes do not have enough elevation to "dial in" bullet-drop correction at extended ranges when used in combination with rainbow cartridges. The term *rainbow* is used to describe the trajectory of a cartridge with substantial bullet drop and the required arc to compensate for the drop (e.g., a .308 Winchester 168-grain load drops approximately 485 inches at 1,000 yards.) These scopes require special angle mounts to achieve dial-in capability at extended ranges.

Precision shooting means eliminating as many variables as possible. In keeping with this line of thinking and to further minimize chances for error in a precision shot, I prefer a fixed-power, a proven second focal plane variable, or a first focal plane reticle scope on the precision rifle. This minimizes the chances of POI shift. Any manufacturer of a high-quality scopes keeps tolerances to a minimum, but they do exist; these tolerances can result in a change of the POI as the scope's magnification is changed. All scopes must be tested and proven prior to duty use.

A popular choice for the fixed-power rifle scope mounted on a police precision rifle is 10x. This may be suitable for medium ranges, but it is inadequate for both close and extended distances.

Shooting statistics indicating that the "average" police rifle shot is approximately 75 yards may make some people content with medium-range performance. Others will view "average" performance as unacceptable. The professional marksman should seek top performance at all ranges that he is expected to cover.

The low-scope-mounted and accurized 5.56mms custom carbine covers most close-to-medium-range requirements, provided that substantial penetration is not required. The scope for the precision rifle should be chosen primarily to cover medium to extended ranges, but both rifles should be capable of overlapping in the medium ranges, which, as we all know, are where the "average" rifle shot takes place. The heavier caliber precision rifle scope should also be capable of focusing down to a very close range so that the more powerful rifle can be used in close-range situations, where penetration beyond that possible with a 5.56mm is required.

The fixed-power tactical scope line from Leupold has gained substantial popularity among professional marksmen. Originally introduced as the Ultra line, it is now known as the Mark 4 line. These scopes feature fixed magnifications, rugged 30mm one-piece tubes, excellent light transmission, waterproofing, and positive click adjustments. These scopes contain extensive elevation adjustment, approximately three times that of standard Leupold scopes. Super-rugged base and ring sets are available for use with these scopes. One optional angle base adds even more elevation adjustment capability, which helps shooters who use rainbow-trajectory calibers for long-range shooting. The elevation adjustability allows shooters to dial in or click in on distant targets. Once you have gathered the proper trajectory information, logged it, and placed it on your turret dial, this method is just as fast as, and more accurate than, the hold over/under method. You will have your own bullet-drop compensator (BDC) finely tuned to the exact "personality" of your rifle and ammo combination. This is more exact than relying on a factory scope's generic BDC for a standard cartridge.

Dialing in requires reliability, which must be tested in each scope considered for duty use. A simple procedure is to zero the rifle at 100 yards and then put up a fresh target 6-inches square with a center aiming point. To check windage and elevation integrity simultaneously, fire one shot into the center aiming point, click the scope down 14 clicks, and then right 14 clicks. While aiming at the center aiming point, fire a three-shot group. Turn the scope up 28 clicks and fire another three-shot group while aiming at the center aiming point. Click the scope left 28 clicks and fire another three-shot group while aiming at the center point. Then click down 28 clicks and fire another three-shot group while aiming at the center. Your next shot should be a single shot aimed at the center of the target after clicking 14 clicks up and 14 clicks right, for a total of 14 shots.

The resulting target pattern from an accurate rifle with a repeatable 1/4-inch click scope would be two shots centered in the aiming point and four tight three-shot groups. The four three-shot groups should be equally just outside your 6-by-6-inch square. If repeatability is determined to be unreliable, the scope should not be used for duty.

A preliminary dry-fire test for scope repeatability would be to install a collimator in the rifle-scope combination that is rigidly held in a rifle vise. Do the same click test while watching cross hair movement in the collimator grid. Log all click stop points to determine whether the pattern is equal. You will need to use a collimator with a grid pattern for this test, not a simple X pattern.

The click adjustments of my Ultra scopes have been determined to be true MOA clicks. Some scopes have 1/4-inch clicks and bill them as MOA clicks. This will cause errors for the long-range shooter who makes distance adjustments based on MOA drop charts.

As stated earlier, MOA is a unit of angular measurement equal to 1.047 inches per

100 yards. This means that 1/4 MOA clicks are worth .261 inch at 100 yards; 1/4-inch clicks, on the other hand, are worth .250 inch at 100 yards. These differences may seem minuscule, but they can add up to sighting errors at extended ranges. The training section of this book provides assistance on how to avoid confusion and errors in this and other areas.

The click adjustments on the Ultra scopes are accomplished by using large, easy-to-operate turrets. The clicks are positive and without much backlash. To ensure that backlash does not create a dialing problem, simply turn the turret two clicks past your selected turret mark and click back two. The MK4 turrets do not feature caps or covers, though I would prefer to have them, but they are O-ring sealed against water.

The turrets feature a single large setscrew for locking the graduated knob on the zero line. This is a big improvement over the standard target scopes that have three very small Allen setscrews that easily strip threads when used regularly. Three of the large setscrews would be an even bigger improvement, but this is not offered by the factory. Custom installation is required to get this extrarugged setup.

Misdialing because of turret slippage (which has not been noted as a problem with the Ultra) could cause serious errors.

The Ultra scopes feature windage and elevation adjustments in the standard locations. Opposite the windage knob there is a third knob located on the left side of the scope, which serves to focus the image and adjust for parallax. The third focus knob eliminates the need for the shooter to make arm movements to the standard AO normally located at the front end of the scope. This is helpful when concealment must be maintained.

The Ultra/MK 4 scopes also come with opaque spring-loaded lens covers, which are highly recommended to protect your scopes' lenses from damage and debris. I prefer see-through, flip-open covers to the opaque style because they allow for observation in foul weather without direct lens contamination. When a precision shot is required, the cover can be flipped open and the lens is exposed to the elements for only a short time.

Whether still wet or dried, rain and snow spots on your lenses can cause substantial sun glare and make target acquisition difficult. In close-range emergency situations the see-through covers can be used in their closed position; although viewing through the plastic caps does not give the clearest sight picture, they are suitable for close, quick shots. Shots from a rifle equipped with opaque scope covers are, of course, to be delayed until the covers are flipped open. This takes time in situations that may not allow for the manipulation.

The Ultras are also supplied with a helpful sunshade. Though this does not solve the problems stemming from a contaminated lens, it reduces the occasions when a contaminated lens causes glare in the shooter's sight picture and decreases the chance of light reflection from the scope lens. Since lenses on the marksman's optics must be considered as possible light reflectors and, therefore, as a marksman's position indicators, a sniper veil over the scope and a porous cloth over the binoculars and spotting scope lenses reduces the chances of reflection. Stretching white gauze over lenses is a common winter camouflage tactic, and tan cheesecloth works well in general conditions. Butler Creek, a scopecap company, has recently introduced plastic lenses in a honeycomb pattern that achieve the same nonreflecting effect.

The coated lens on your high-quality (expensive) scope must be protected and cared for if proper performance is expected. The best cleaning products for scope lenses should be available from either the scope manufacturer or a full-service camera store. Quality camera-lens-cleaning equipment works well.

Rule of thumb: Keep your lens caps closed at all times when they are not actually required to be open. This is especially true when cleaning the weapon: solvent splatter on the lens can destroy the lens coatings.

The Ultra scope line was originally introduced in fixed magnifications of 10x, 16x, and 20x. Recently the 20x models have been hard to find because they have been dropped from the line.

Fixed-scope magnification for the precision rifle is an area for serious evaluation. Introducing a reliable variable MK4 scope in the 4–20x range with

The Leupold Ultra scopes have proven to be high-quality units. Quadruple-ring mounting (bottom) increases scope-tube protection and rigidity.

tactical reticle and an adjustable light feature would solve many problems. Letters to the company may help.

With a scoped carbine available to handle the closer ranges, the chances of having to use the precision rifle closer than 50 to 75 yards are slim but not impossible. Be prepared for close-range encounters where heavier caliber penetration may be required. At extended ranges, higher magnification will be useful in target identification and shot placement. Remembering that the precision rifle's scope has a fixed power, the magnification should not be so great that the scope's use is negated at the medium overlapping distances. The Ultra scope-focusing feature addresses this issue very well: even the higher magnifications will focus down to approximately 15 yards. The field of view is small, but the image is clear.

The magnification debate over what works best can be kept somewhat limited if you accept the two-rifle concept. The distances at which precision-rifle use may be expected are medium to longer ranges, which allow for a more powerful, higher-magnification scope.

The higher magnifications make the image appear larger, hence easier to identify and place the shot. The drawbacks to higher magnification are (1) smaller FOV and increased magnification of any existent shooter movement, (2) extreme magnifications that may result in image distortion from magnification of atmospheric conditions, and (3) scope images that may appear darker in low light because of decreased light transmission. Only top-quality scopes with coated lenses should be considered.

After considering the drawbacks to higher magnifications, some rifle instructors follow the military's lead and favor medium-powered scopes in the 10x range. Many cite the difficulty in off-hand shooting with the higher powered scopes. It is true that some shooters have more difficulty locating and holding their targets with higher powered scopes, especially when firing off hand. Getting back on target quickly after the shot also requires more skill because the higher-magnification scopes have a smaller FOV. I believe, however, that proper training overcomes these difficulties and allows the shooter to benefit from higher magnification. The tactical marksman is held to positive ID standards, and the added magnification is helpful in meeting this requirement.

Where off-hand holding of the target is concerned, wavering around the target is not precision shooting. Any unsupported shooting in critical situations should be a last resort, limited to the closer ranges, and probably more suited to the carbine. The carbine's light weight, accuracy, and quick handling make it a better choice in makeshift shooting positions.

Very important rule of thumb: Always have enough support to make a successful shot. A hurried miss and good intentions do not meet performance standards.

I have had good results with extended-range, precision-rifle, fixed-scope magnification in the 20x range. I prefer not to go below 16x, nor above 24x (a custom power boost may now be required to increase magnification of Ultra scopes beyond 16x). This seems to be a good compromise range of fixed magnification, because it allows for target ID and close-range emergency shots. Magnification below 16x begins to produce problems in positive facial identification at longer ranges. Magnification above 24x in a fixed-power scope makes the FOV extremely small in a close-range emergency shot.

Substantial firing of a rifle equipped with a higher magnification scope causes the heat waves that emanate from the rifle's barrel to be visible in the shooter's sight picture. This can be a distraction unless a heat shield is used from the scope lens to the muzzle. This would not be a problem on the majority of actual call-outs because of the very limited number of rounds usually fired. But in training, observing barrel heat waves should remind you that heat is a primary factor in barrel wear and that the barrel should be allowed to cool, and possibly cleaned, before firing is resumed.

The best way to evaluate your magnification needs is to test scopes under your individual conditions. This will allow you to weigh the pros and cons of scopes of the middle to higher magnifications in your environmental and probable call-out conditions. Higher power scopes will not only show barrel heat but also mirage conditions. Experienced shooters can obtain visible wind information by reading the mirage; those less experienced may find sighting interference disturbing.

Confrontation with an experienced rifleman may force you to outdistance him. Make sure your equipment and training allow you to do so.

Should you decide on a higher fixed-magnification scope, you must understand that it takes more training to acquire targets in the sight picture and reduce perceived shooter shake. Once this is understood, you can benefit from the advantages of the higher powered scopes and the simplicity of fixed magnification.

A variable-powered scope with first focal plane reticle is a solution for the tactical marksman looking for the best magnification for the shot at hand, without having to worry about POI displacement. First focal plane scopes are becoming increasingly available in the United States and are worth looking into. The variety of magnification ranges gives excellent coverage of the marksman's area of responsibility.

First focal plane reticle scopes with variable-magnification ranges normally require a custom scope order. Customized Leupold target scopes are available with first focal plane reticles and variable magnification. They are reliable and work well for those who are not distracted by the variable-reticle size.

Large scope manufacturers and custom scope shops offer multiple-reticle patterns and styles that meet the tactical marksman's special requirements. I have designed an uncluttered tactical reticle that assists the shooter with range estimation, windage holds, and target leads.

A D & L customized AR-15 mounted with a PVS4 night-vision device. The free-floating barrel allows the use of the bipod without affecting point of impact. By adding a flash suppressor on a night rifle you can use a night scope without the "blooming" effect a muzzle flash can create.

NIGHT VISION

In specialized operations, a night-vision (NV) sight is quite helpful, but, believe it or not, the majority of urban police night tactical operations do not require NV devices (NVDs).

NV scopes are available in numerous reticle patterns to suit specific applications. The ANPVS4 NV sight even has operator-changeable reticles for different projectiles. Even the latest NV sights are somewhat bulky and have low magnification and coarse aiming points. This makes them better suited to closer ranges on a dedicated night rifle, such as a 20-inch, low-scoped AR-15.

Ranging reticles in NVDs are essential if extended ranges are encountered; visual estimation of range at night is difficult. NVDs with range finders commonly range to 1,000 meters: being able to range out to 1,000 meters is helpful in determining how much further you have to travel, but shooting at such distances without positive target identification is unacceptable for the tactical marksman. A more logical use of the commonly available low-magnification NV sight is at close to medium ranges with a point-blank zero, and where positive target ID can be ensured.

Mounting hardware for NVDs, even the "guaranteed return to zero" mounts,

The Simrad NVD mounts on the objective lens of the day scope. This enhances the marksman's night-shooting capability without his having to carry a separate night scope-mounted rifle.

cannot be trusted in live encounters. QD mounts normally return to "almost" zero; this is unacceptable to the tactical marksman. Zero *must* remain precise, which means that if a standard NV sight is going to be issued to a marksman for special operations, it must be mounted on a separate rifle. This also means more training and more ammunition. A full-time tactical marksman may be able to keep current with three rifles, but for a part-time officer it may be too time consuming. Departments should be realistic and as uncomplicated as possible in the equipment issued to its personnel, especially those who have limited time to train. Top performance with more than two rifles takes substantially more training time. Being only marginally familiar with any piece of equipment is unwise—and potentially dangerous.

The size and weight of most NVDs are more than those for conventional scopes, and add bulk to your rifle. The tactical officer who limits his NVD use to the close to medium ranges should mount the device on a less cumbersome midrange carbine to avoid the awkwardness of the larger precision rifle weighted down with a NVD.

The reticle pattern for the NVD-rifle combination should be simple and uncluttered for quick use at closer ranges. The combination should be set up with a point-blank zero to avoid having to make manual scope adjustments in dark, critical situations.

A carbine with an effective flash suppressor will almost completely eliminate NVD "blooming," common on NVD-equipped rifles without flash suppressors. Blooming subjects the shooter's eyes to a bright flash of light in the scope's sight picture at the instant of discharge. This results in a temporary reduction in the shooter's night vision. Some NVDs may experience a brief shutdown when used on a rifle with noticeable muzzle flash. This is the scope's way of protecting itself from the harsh

You can obtain nighttime range estimation by attaching Simrad NVDs to laser range finders. Simrad KN200F on LP7 laser range finder.

light flash. Although this feature may prolong the life of the scope, it makes aimed, rapid follow-up shots impossible.

Recent developments in NVDs have made them more compact, practical, and efficient. Dedicated NVDs must be mounted on a dedicated night rifle to ensure proper zero retention. NVDs that supplement day scopes allow the tactical marksman to use the two-rifle concept, thus eliminating the need for a third rifle dedicated to a NVD. The units that currently show the most promise for the tactical officer are ones that mount on the objective bell of the standard day rifle scope. To acquire an aiming point, they use the day scope's reticle, as well as the scope's turret adjustments. The marksman can carry the device in his field gear and attach it to the scope as needed. Manufacturers claim that this attachment is possible without affecting the day zero, but this needs to be tested thoroughly before buying this expensive item.

The manufacturers also advise using these units on lower powered scopes (10x and below) for best light transmission and less grainy sight picture. This is another consideration when selecting a day scope, if you plan to supplement it with this type of NVD. By properly selecting equipment you can increase its versatility.

Teleranger with Simrad KN250F.

DAY SCOPES

Day scopes with lighted reticles have been around for several years, and tactical officers could make good use of them. Often, high-quality optics permit identification of a target in low light, but there is a problem: when a black cross hair is placed on a dark target, the target obscures the cross hair. In recent years, scopes have incorporated luminous cross hairs, lighted centers, and dots to counter this problem.

I have evaluated numerous scopes with these features and found problems with

Simrad units are adaptable to a variety of weapons.

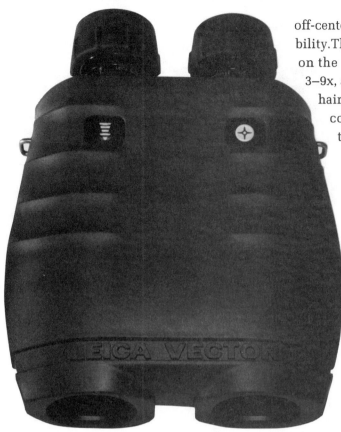

Leica has developed a combination range finder, binocular, and compass in one compact unit. This unit is considered a class I laser product.

off-center dots, parallax, clarity, and overall quality and reliability. The best units are Zeiss and Oakshore, which work well on the midrange carbine and are available in 1–5x, 2–7x, 3–9x, and 3–12x magnifications. The dot size or illuminated hair is precise, and the intensity is adjustable to existing conditions. In daylight, the dot does not need to be turned on because the standard black cross hairs are always visible.

The Zeiss unit is excellent quality throughout, and the price reflects it: approximately $1,750. Currently the only Zeiss scope with the selective reticle light is the 3–12x 56mm. This is a large scope, approximately 15 inches long. The 56mm works well on the custom AR scope mounting rail, but the 56mm objective lens scope normally sits too high on bolt guns.

The electric dot sights featuring only an electronic aiming point are unsuitable for tactical operations. This type of electronic sight is currently used in IPSC and similar competitions and has proved to be unreliable at its current state of development. If the electronic circuitry or batteries on these units fail, the tactical marksman will be left without any reticle; but a scope with a selective reticle light provides for standard day cross hair backup in event of such failure.

LASERS

Laser sights actually project the aiming point onto the target; however, contrary

High-tech laser range finder.

to what you see on television and in movies, actual field use of the currently available sights has proven them to be highly overrated for general operations. Without special goggles, the aiming point is virtually invisible under sunlight conditions. In artificial light and darkness, the aiming point is visible but does nothing to illuminate or identify the target. In smoke, gas, rain, or snow, the beam can actually be tracked back to the shooter's position.

When the dot is projected onto a distant target, it covers too large an area for precision shooting. The projected dot also magnifies the shooter's shake and makes most shooters hesitant to shoot. A person well trained in more conventional shooting skills can normally outperform the laser-aimed shooter easily; this is especially true with handgun-mounted lasers.

You achieve top shooting performance through top-quality equipment and proper training, not gizmos and gadgets.

Lasers mounted on full-stocked submachine guns and supplemented with a white light for target identification can be effective for close-range entry work. Submachine guns so equipped and used from the underarm assault position facilitate identifying targets and acquiring a precise aiming point. This shooting position works well in close quarters when the shooter must don a gas mask, making standard shoulder-mounted sighting difficult. It also allows for good weapon retention. Firing accurately with this technique takes training and practice, especially in locating the dot. Laser and light mounting can make a firearm less rugged, bulkier, and battery dependent, and require laser-zero and standard sight confirmations as well. Don't overcomplicate your weapons to the point that they become unreliable.

Laser sights seem to appeal to the inexperienced shooter looking to buy performance instead of training to achieve it. My use of lasers has indicated that, at their current state of development, their use as a gun sight is limited to very special applications. Proper technique is much more valuable to the shooter than overrated laser sights.

Firearm-mounted lasers do work well as training aids, however. They give visual feedback to the shooter about how much an incorrect trigger pull influences his shot placement: he can see the dot move off target when he pulls the trigger.

The area in which lasers are most valuable for the tactical marksman is range finding. Modern laser range finders are the approximate size of a set of field binoculars and are available in a variety of power levels, suited for both close and long ranges. The modern, compact laser range finder is accurate and practical in the field. Self-contained scope, laser range finder, and angle indicator units are in the testing stages. The primary drawback is the cost. Depending

Laser sights are best for special-entry applications and training roles. Lasers provide an aiming point, but "white" lights are better for target identification.

on the manufacturer, availability, and power range, prices range anywhere from $500 to $20,000.

As with any laser device, no matter what the power rating, they should not be directed into undeserving eyes.

CONVENTIONAL SCOPES

More conventional scope reticles feature various extrafine, fine, medium, and coarse aiming-point patterns. Center dots, mil dots, and custom dot pattern reticles are available, along with a multitude of thick- and thin-post reticles. Range-finding scope reticles are available, from the simple to the complicated and cluttered.

By following a simple guideline when selecting a reticle pattern for a tactical scope, you can eliminate undesirable reticles. A reticle should allow for precise shot placement over a broad range of light conditions and assist in range determination without complicating the sight picture. This simple guideline alone will eliminate thick-post reticles, extrafine reticles with and without a center dot, and coarse cross hair reticles. Extrafine cross hairs tend to fade out of view under bright light and low-light conditions; this is true with either a center black dot or no dot.

Blunt-post and coarse cross hair reticles cover up too much of the target for precise shot placement.

Stadia wire reticles designed for use in range determination actually place multiple, full-length cross intersections in the sight picture. There should be only one full-length cross hair intersection (aiming point) in the entire sight picture in order to avoid any confusion when a quick sight picture is acquired. Scopes featuring stadia wires will often incorporate a BDC elevation turret. Because these generic BDCs seldom equate to the trajectory of a specific load in a specific environment, they are of questionable value.

Standard fine duplex, duplex hash mark (etched reticle only), duplex mil dot, and logical custom dot pattern reticles work well on the precision tactical rifle. Standard fine duplex or medium duplex works well on the midrange carbine. The selective cross hair light would be a good addition on either unit. (Drop a friendly letter to the scope companies and request this feature, along with rubber armoring. Maybe demonstrated shooter interest in these features can get the manufacturers interested.)

The duplex cross hair features thicker lines near the outer portion of the reticle. The center of the duplex reticle features fine hairs for precise aiming. In low light or glare conditions, the thicker outer portion of the cross hairs will stay visible and allow centering of the finer center portion of the reticle. In daylight conditions, the thicker outer cross hairs appear to draw the shooter's eye to the center of the reticle, where focus should be centered.

A fine duplex, duplex hash mark, mil dot, or custom dot pattern can assist in ranging and compensating for wind drift and bullet drop. These styles of reti-

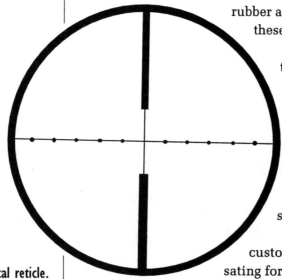

The D & L tactical reticle.

cles are the most logical choice for a precision tactical rifle, and proper application of these reticles provide excellent performance. I have designed two custom reticle patterns for tactical use. One is in current production on a custom order basis. The reticles assist the shooter in range determination, wind drift hold-off, and leading targets.

THE D & L TACTICAL RETICLE PATTERN (DOT PATTERN)

The D & L tactical reticle pattern assists the shooter with range estimation, wind drift hold-off, and leading targets. The duplex vertical cross hair can be positioned with its thick-to-thin section at the top of the target, and notations can be made as to where the center cross hair is positioned on the target. The farther away the target, the farther down the intersection will be on the target. Another range estimation feature is the dot placement on the horizontal cross hair. At 100 yards, the distance between the dots is 3 inches. This means that bracketing a 6-inch target, such as a facing head target, between the center two dots indicates that the target is at 100 yards. Bracketing a 6-inch target between the vertical cross hair and the first dot indicates that the target is 200 yards away. A 6-inch target bracketed by the first dot and past the vertical cross hair halfway to the other centermost dot would be 150 yards away.

With this pattern, the elevation turret is used to click in correct elevation for the range indicated. Since wind drift has a varying effect and is constantly changing,

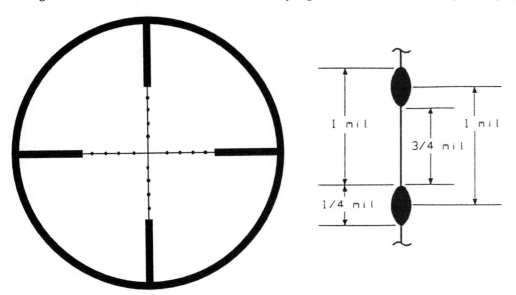

Left, the mil-dot reticle.

Right, close-up of mil-dot dimensions and spacing in the reticle.

The mil-dot reticle was placed in service by the U.S. Marine Corps in the late 1970s as a range estimation aid. Its name comes from the term millradian and the reticle dot that is spaced in one mil increments on the crosswire. A mil formula allows the shooter to calculate a table based on the size of the object being estimated. The formula is as follows:

$$\frac{\text{Height or width of target (in yards)} \times 1{,}000}{\text{Height or width of target (in mils)}} = \text{Range (in yards)}$$

Once he has a chart, the shooter can estimate the size of the target in inches and locate that figure across the top of the chart.

hold-off is simpler for windage compensation. At 100 yards, holding one dot over from center allows for 3 inches of wind drift. Holding two dots over from center gives you 6 inches of wind drift compensation. Holding one dot over from center at 200 yards give you 6 inches of wind drift compensation, and so on. The dots on the horizontal line also serve as excellent reference points when leading targets.

The D & L duplex hash mark pattern works similarly to this dot pattern, but the various sizes of the vertical hash marks give a 10-inch reference line from 100 to 1,000 yards. This reticle would require an etched glass reticle to produce.

Inches =	9	12	16	18	20	22	24	28	32	36	60	66	69	72
3/4	333	444	593	666	741	815	889	1037	1185	1333	2223	2444	2556	2667
1	250	333	445	500	556	611	667	778	889	1000	1667	1833	1917	2000
1 1/4	200	266	355	400	445	489	534	622	711	800	1334	1466	1537	1600
1 1/2	167	222	396	333	371	407	445	519	593	667	1111	1222	1278	1333
1 3/4	143	190	254	285	318	349	381	445	508	571	953	1047	1095	1143
2	125	167	222	250	278	306	334	389	445	500	834	917	959	1000
2 1/4	111	148	197	222	247	272	296	446	395	444	741	815	852	889
2 1/2	100	133	178	200	222	244	267	311	356	400	667	733	767	800
2 3/4	91	121	161	182	202	222	243	283	323	364	606	667	697	727
3	83	111	148	167	185	204	222	259	296	333	556	611	639	667
3 1/4	77	102	137	154	171	188	205	239	273	308	513	564	590	615
3 1/2	71	95	127	143	159	175	191	222	254	286	476	524	548	571
3 3/4	67	89	118	133	148	163	178	207	237	267	445	489	511	533
4	63	83	111	125	139	153	167	195	222	250	417	458	479	500
4 1/4	59	78	104	118	131	144	157	183	209	235	392	431	451	471
4 1/2	56	74	99	111	124	136	148	173	197	222	370	407	426	445
4 3/4	53	70	93	105	117	128	140	164	187	210	351	386	404	421
5	50	67	89	100	111	122	133	156	178	200	333	367	383	400
5 1/4	48	63	85	95	105	116	127	148	169	190	318	349	365	381
5 1/2	45	61	81	91	101	111	121	141	162	182	303	333	349	364
5 3/4	43	58	77	87	97	106	116	135	155	174	290	319	333	348
6	42	56	74	83	93	102	111	130	148	167	278	306	320	333
6 1/4	40	53	71	80	89	98	107	124	142	160	267	293	307	320
6 1/2	38	51	68	77	86	94	103	120	137	154	256	282	295	308
6 3/4	37	49	66	74	82	91	99	115	132	148	247	272	284	296
7	36	48	63	71	79	87	95	111	127	143	238	262	274	286
8	31	42	56	63	70	76	83	97	111	125	208	229	240	250
9	28	37	49	56	62	68	74	86	99	111	185	203	213	222
10	25	33	44	50	56	61	67	79	89	100	167	183	192	200

Measure the height or width of the target in mils and locate the correct figure on the left side of the chart. Follow the chart in from the left and down from the top to locate the range of the target.

MIL DOT RETICLE PATTERN

The mil dot reticle is popular in some military tactical scopes. The known dimensions of the scope assist the shooter in making range estimations and hold-off calculations. One mil equals 1 yard at 1,000 yards. The center-to-center distance between each dot on the scope is 1 mil. Using this information, the shooter can calculate distances. The shooter has to be well trained in the use of the mil dot to avoid miscalculations. I prefer simpler methods to reduce the chances of human error.

RANGE ESTIMATION

I have not found the current BDCs adequate for the tactical marksman. They may work well for general military applications, where center mass hits are sufficient, but the tactical officer usually requires more precision.

The BDCs may be set up for the same cartridge you are shooting, but variations between rifles, ammo, bullet weights, velocity, and shooting conditions always seem to make the POI a little different from the point of aim (POA). The best solution for achieving quick, precise bullet-drop compensation is to make your own calibrated scope turret. You must use the specific rifle-ammo-scope combination for which you are gathering information, and collect your range data in the environment in which you expect to be deployed. Translate this information into your data book and directly onto your scope turret. All of this extra effort will take substantial data development time on the range, but the results from this kind of extra effort are what will separate you from the ordinary rifleman.

The low-scoped, midrange carbine set up with a top-quality duplex pattern scope and a point-blank zero will require regular zero confirmation only when used within its intended distances. The extended-range precision rifle performs best when it is dialed in to the correct distances. This requires that a quality, repeatable scope be rigidly mounted to the precision rifle and that a lot of range time be expended in developing the data or "dope" book. (See Chapter 9 on training.)

Before dialing in at extended distances, you must know several things, one of which is the distance to the target. This information, along with the bullet's trajectory, wind drift, and other shooting conditions, will assist you in calculating the proper scope settings to make single-shot hits.

Accurate range estimation can easily mean the difference between hitting and missing. For example: you are shooting at a 600-yard target, but you miscalculate the range to be 500 yards. Provided you do everything else right, your 168-grain BTHP .308 Winchester Match round (traveling 2,500-fps muzzle velocity with elevation at 4,500 feet) will strike 40.2 inches low. Distance estimations are difficult for most people, especially at extended distance, so use of proper range-finding equipment and technique is advised. Given the present availability of equipment, top quality also means top dollar.

Rough range finding can be accomplished by various visual and reticle comparison procedures. However, these procedures should be used as a supplement to dedicated distance-finding equipment, thus allowing you to compare range estimates. The final range reading should be obtained from your proven precision range finder. Compare the results with your visual distance average, and apply your most accurate

The Barr and Stroud range finder is an excellent investment for the precision marksman. Conversion data from meters to yards, calibrations, and maintenance information for the range finder can be carried in the data bag. Laser units are more portable but extremely expensive.

range estimate to your scope turret. Such comparisons show you how accurate your range-finding skills are and how much you need to improve them. If you should ever find yourself without a working range finder, your visual skills will be needed.

Precision range finding requires precision equipment, and the farther you intend to shoot accurately, the more you need the equipment. Long-range precision shooting is not "walking them in there," but it is calculated shooting intended to make one hit with one shot.

State-of-the-art laser range-finding equipment is probably the quickest, most portable, and most accurate (as well as expensive) equipment available. A less than state-of-the-art range finder popular among distance shooters is the World War II-era artillery model, which was most commonly made in Germany or Britain and used for artillery adjustment. The two models most commonly located are capable of ranging from between 250 to 20,000 yards and 500 to 20,000 yards. These optical units work on a coincidence principle, typically accurate to plus or minus 5 yards at 1,000 yards, giving them acceptable accuracy within rifle-shooting distances.

These units have three drawbacks: price (though not as much as the latest laser models), availability, and bulk. They are not pocket models, measuring approximately 3 feet in length and 2 1/2 inches in diameter, and weighing approximately 5 pounds.

On the plus side, they feature fine 14x optics, are not battery dependent, and can be user-calibrated to ensure accuracy. For an extended-range rifleman without the funds for a state-of-the-art laser, the optical range finder is an excellent choice.

Cheap plastic range finders commonly marketed to hunters are not worth the paper they are packaged in. Buy top-quality or save your hard-earned money.

ESTIMATING ENVIRONMENTAL CONDITIONS

Wind Drift

Computer calculations of a bullet's wind drift have come a long way in recent years. Obtaining an accurate printout for your rifle and cartridge combination under specific conditions gives you valuable information to confirm and add to your data book for field use. To make accurate use of this information, you must establish wind speed and direction. You must understand that the wind speed where you are and the wind speed where the long-distance target is are probably different; you have to be accurate on your end and be able to estimate downrange wind activity. The marksman should also understand that the wind's influence on the bullet's drift will be greater if started at the shooter's location rather than at some point downrange because the wind has more time and distance to affect the projectile. The downrange wind, however, is acting against a bullet with reduced velocity.

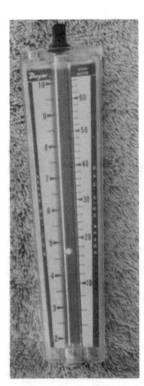

A digital turbine wind meter is a great aid in calculating wind drift compensation. A turbine meter is more accurate, but also more expensive, than a plastic gauge-style meter. An accurate, rugged digital temperature-humidity meter provides additional shot-calculating information. Though not as accurate, wristwatch-size atmospheric condition indicators (not shown) are becoming increasingly common and affordable.

Using a top-quality portable wind meter reduces wind speed estimation errors. In this case top-quality means rugged and accurate, such as a digital turbine model. They are small, hand-held, accurate, and expensive. V-shaped plastic units with the little ball and gauge inside, commonly found on the competition rifle shooting circuits, are of questionable value.

Basic shooting skills should already be mastered before shooters venture into advanced marksmanship. Experienced shooters believe that accurate range and wind estimations are often the most critical factors to a successful shot. Wind drift

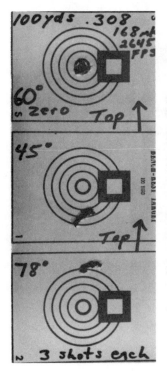

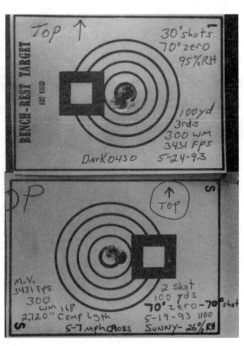

Atmospheric condition changes should be taken into consideration for your specific rifle and ammunition. It is not uncommon for a 20-degree change in the middle temperature range to change the .308's POI one full MOA. The two .300 WM targets indicate POI change.

(Top right) You should always take extra batteries and important data to the field with you.

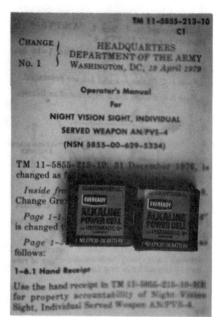

(Above and Right) The initial "go" gear should be kept as portable as possible to expedite quick responses. More elaborate post equipment can be packed in later if a semipermanent post is to be established.

Hard cases that might be carried into field operations should not be reflective aluminum. "Sandbags" filled with Styrofoam beads are much easier to "hump" than the real sand.

A top-quality hard case is required for rigorous precision-rifle transport. If possible, keep your rifle with you in the passenger cabin during air travel. This minimizes any air-pressure effects on your system.

(Below) Precision .22 rimfire rifles work well for light elimination.

estimation is the most critical because bullet trajectory remains fairly constant. I have previously discussed errors caused by poor range estimation; poor wind drift estimation can cause at least as many, if not more, problems for the long-range shooter. Without the best of equipment and wind-estimation techniques, a shooter firing a .308 Winchester 168-grain

BTHP could be off the 500-yard mark by approximately 20 inches if he makes just a 10 mph-miscalculation.

Just as with range estimation, your wind-estimating equipment, technique, and experience should all complement one other. Make your visible estimate at your location based on your surroundings (e.g., felt air movement, observed vegetation movement, smoke drift). Then, compare your estimate with an accurate wind meter. Look downrange for environmental indicators of wind speed and direction. Compare these with your immediate surroundings. If they appear the same, you may be able to use your wind meter reading to calculate drift as a constant all the way to the target. If the wind patterns do not look constant, you will have to call on your experience to compensate for the difference.

Temperature and Humidity

Temperature and humidity play important roles in making your bullet do different things in flight. Monitoring these conditions will assist you in making any necessary compensations. Accurate readings mean

BENCH-REST TARGET

50 yds   100 YARD   5 rds

DEL 10-22 custom
Benchrest 22 LR

(Right) Portable lighting is required for the marksman wanting to extend his day scope's capability into darkness.

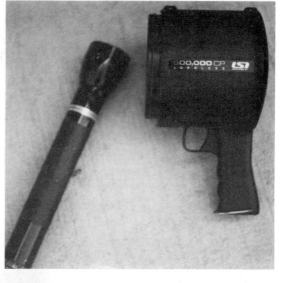

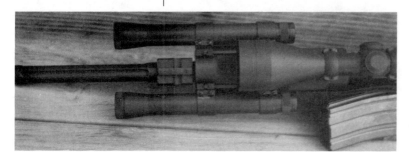

Some companies offer high-intensity lights that attach to the scope. A shooter will have to evaluate his individual requirements and select a light accordingly. I prefer self-contained lights to those that require external wiring to a power source. I don't recommend direct light-to-scope attachment because any impact the light may sustain could be transferred to the scope.

(Below) A top-quality collimator is a valuable tool for the tactical marksman.

using accurate equipment. Rugged and very portable temperature/ humidity meters are suitable for your "go" bag. More on these effects in later chapters.

Nighttime Conditions

Portable, powerful, self-contained spotlights are invaluable additions to any tactical marksman's post equipment. They allow for target illumination, distraction, and identification, while avoiding the expense of NVDs. However, to avoid exposure, the spotlights must be operated remotely and backlighting must be avoided. Powerful spotlights make accurate shooting possible at more than 300 yards during nighttime; standard rechargeable spotlights, at 200 yards; and modern rechargeable duty flashlights, at 100 yards.

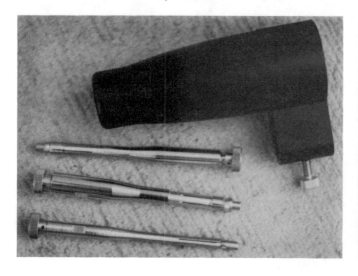

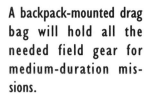

A backpack-mounted drag bag will hold all the needed field gear for medium-duration missions.

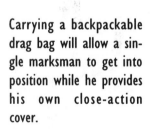

Carrying a backpackable drag bag will allow a single marksman to get into position while he provides his own close-action cover.

D & L designed Kydex holsters are state of the art for backup weapon carry.

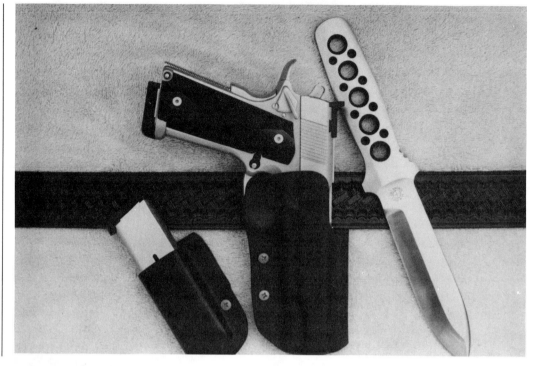

(Below) A top-quality suppressor, such as this Thundertrap model, can reduce the initial report of a centerfire rifle to less than that of a .22 LR. Felt recoil is also reduced. Photo by Doug Anderson.

(Right) A CQB suppressor on a 5.56mm carbine. Photo by Doug Anderson.

Auxiliary lighting that is attachable to the midrange carbine is extremely beneficial. However, the light must not be mounted on the barrel because this affects POI. I prefer not to attach auxiliary lights directly to the scope because any impact on the light could be transmitted to the scope. The light(s) should be self-contained, free of any outside wiring, and bright. Quality forearm-mounted lights and a rifle scope will allow accurate shooting at more than 100 yards at night. The lights also make the midrange carbine suitable for low-light entry work. A lighted weapon will, of course, indicate the shooter's location, and must be used accordingly (i.e., shoot and move).

Collimators

The collimator is a very valuable tool for the tactical marksman and will be covered in detail in later chapters. Quality is again a primary selection consideration: your collimator should feature a fine grid pattern for use in plotting your zeros; a simple bore sight with an X reticle is not suitable.

Adjustable spuds are recommended for the collimator. This will allow the spud to be placed in the bore, then snugged in place, thereby eliminating any rifling damage caused by trying to force an oversized solid spud in the bore. If your rifle has a muzzle brake, be sure the spuds are long enough to solidly seat in the bore.

OTHER EQUIPMENT

You should use a drag bag or some form of carry pack/garment for deploying your precision rifle system in the field. This frees your hands for carbine operation on close encounters. Your carry pack should also be equipped with field camouflage and related post equipment items for your specific environment. These items may include the following:

A PV510 day/night vision scope mounted on a MR-30PG.

- Ammunition (rifle, carbine, pistol)
- Aspirin
- Backup data book
- Ballistic vest
- Binoculars
- Bipod
- Camo paint
- Climbing gear
- Cold/hot/rain gear
- Compass
- Cord or rope
- Dog and/or insect repellent
- Expedient post camouflage
- Extra batteries
- Fire fly
- First aid equipment
- Flares
- Food
- Gas mask
- Ghillie suit

- Glass cutter
- Ground pad
- Handgun
- Hedge clippers
- Knife
- Map
- Microcassette recorder
- Minisaw
- MREs
- Night trail markers
- Perimeter security devices
- Periscope
- Poncho
- Radio
- Range finder
- Sanitation supplies
- Sleeping bag
- Smoke grenades
- Snap links (carabiners)
- Still and video camera
- Strobe light
- Tape
- Water
- Water-purification tablets
- Waterproof notebook and pencil
- Wire cutters

SUMMARY

In selecting optics and related equipment, you must make choices based on your individual requirements, keeping in mind that reliable performance is priority one. Don't shortchange yourself in quality or distance. Reliably outreaching your target may be your safest option.

In 2000, Leupold brought out a selective illuminated reticle scope. Here is a 3-10X on a D&L PPC (Professional Perimeter Carbine).

Ballistics and Ammunition

BALLISTICS IS THE SCIENCE OF PROJECTILES IN MOTION AND CAN BE BROKEN DOWN into three parts for thorough understanding: internal, external, and terminal. Provided that the shooter's rifle was built with uniform accuracy in mind and that the rifleman understands the need for human consistency while shooting, the last two parts are more important than the first one. However, complete understanding of all three is essential for top performance.

INTERNAL BALLISTICS

Internal ballistics concern the activity inside the rifle from the time of cartridge ignition until the bullet leaves the end of the barrel. This period is extremely brief, but critical to the accuracy achieved downrange: bullets that do not depart the rifle uniformly will not deliver consistent accuracy on target.

Ignition of a cartridge in a rifle chamber takes place when the trigger is squeezed and the sear releases the hammer or striker. The firing pin or striker is driven forward by spring pressure and hits the primer, thus igniting the priming compound. The primer itself consists of a cup containing explosive compound covered by a paper foil disk. The primer's anvil sits on top of the disk. The firing pin strike on the primer cup crushes the priming compound against the anvil, causing detonation. Primer detonation in turn ignites the powder charge. Combustion of the powder charge creates energy very rapidly. Confining this energy inside the rifle's chamber creates pressure seeking escape. The pressure expands the cartridge case, which acts to seal the chamber. The pressure obtains its exit path of least resistance by pushing the bullet down the barrel. Provided that properly loaded concentric cartridge cases are used, the case expansion will be consistent, and the bullet will start in proper alignment with the rifling of the barrel. Nonconcentric bullet entry into the rifling will cause bullet deformation and a bullet that exits the muzzle while spinning out of line with its longitude axis. On-target accuracy suffers substantially if this occurs.

A true action and true action-to-barrel alignment are critical for accuracy.

65

The pressure that expands the cartridge case and drives the bullet down the barrel also forces the case head back against the bolt face. This action in turn forces the locking lugs back into the locking recesses inside the receiver. If the case-head is not square with the bolt face, or the locking lugs are not equally seated in the receiver, the unequal impact will exert unequal force on the receiver. Unequal force on the receiver generates unequal vibration on the barrel. Unequal or inconsistent force will cause shot dispersion. Uniformity is the key to accuracy and is attained through properly fitted rifle components, match ammunition, and proper shooter technique.

Routine barrel vibration is caused by the bullet's entry into the rifling. Because the bullet is larger in diameter than the barrel's bore, the bullet is pushed into the bore and engraved by the rifling, which imparts spin to the bullet. The oversized bullet interacting with the undersized lands creates longitudinal barrel vibrations, while the rearward recoil force and stock impact on the shooter generate barrel whip or vertical barrel vibrations. The rifling-imparted spin on the bullet as it travels down the barrel creates yet another vibration on the barrel—torsional vibration.

Barrel whip can be minimized by using stiff barrels and keeping the rearward recoil force in as straight a line as possible. Bull barrels, proper shooting position, and straight-line stocks help accomplish this. Erratic shooting positions with varying degrees of grip or sling pressure, along with any barrel or bedding inconsistencies, can generate lateral barrel vibrations.

The vibrations imparted to the barrel during the firing of a cartridge continue while the bullet speeds down the barrel. The barrel actually moves around its longitudinal axis while the bullet travels through it. The vibrations create a barrel whip pattern commonly referred to as nodes and antinodes: high points of the whip pattern are antinodes, and low points are nodes. The antinode portions of the pattern are the points of most movement.

An area of critical concern for the rifleman seeking accuracy is the bullet's release point: the end of the barrel, or the muzzle. Unfortunately, studies indicate the end of the barrel is always an area of highest whip, or antinode, when a shot is fired.

Creating bullet-release consistency is a high priority for gunsmiths building rifles for accuracy; such gunsmiths have learned that rigidity minimizes barrel whip. Larger diameter barrels increase rigidity, thus minimizing barrel whip. The combination of a superior-quality rigid barrel properly fitted to a trued action with a noninterfering stock provides consistent bullet release. Superior-quality ammunition matched to the rifle and correct noninterfering shooter technique delivers the desired on-target accuracy. Inadequacy in any of these areas leads to less than top performance.

EXTERNAL BALLISTICS

External ballistics is of critical concern to the tactical rifleman. You must know what your bullet does from the time it leaves the muzzle until it arrives at the target. Without this knowledge, your attempts to intersect your bullet with the target will be unreliable. Quite often a miss is blamed on inadequate basic marksmanship skills when, in reality, it was a misunderstanding of the bullet's trajectory or drift that caused the miss. A combination of advanced personal shooting ability, mind-set, mechanically accurate tools, and ballistic knowledge makes a professional marksman.

A bullet exiting the muzzle is immediately confronted with two influences: gravity and air resistance. Gravity acts to pull the bullet down, while air resistance forces a reduction of the bullet's forward motion. Gravity is a constant force; whereas the effect of air resistance can be decreased by aerodynamic bullet shape.

Contrary to popular belief, the bullet does not gain velocity and elevation just outside the muzzle of a level rifle. In fact, the bullet may actually lose velocity inside the rifle's barrel if the incorrect barrel length was chosen for the cartridge's powder-burning rate: barrel length beyond the point where peak pressure is developed simply results in friction.

Gravity acts upon the bullet as soon as it exits the muzzle. Since the sightline is above the bore, the gravity's action requires raising the angle of the bullet's muzzle departure to make the bullet intersect with the line of sight. The upward angle of the bullet's departure and the downward gravitational pull on the bullet create an arc or a curve—the bullet's trajectory. Because different cartridges are capable of different trajectories, you must evaluate what best suits your needs. Cartridges often become known as "rainbow guns" or "flat shooters," based on their trajectory.

The time the bullet takes to reach the target is known as the time of flight, which is determined by the velocity of the bullet and influences its trajectory. For example, a bullet with twice the velocity will arrive on target twice as fast; this means that there is only one-half as much time for gravity to act on the bullet, resulting in a flatter trajectory. A flatter trajectory, in turn, means the bullet can be kept closer to the line of sight and that the chances of shot placement error are reduced. A faster bullet also reduces the time for the wind to drift its POI.

Air resistance is another important factor that affects a bullet in flight. The high-velocity projectile forces the air in front of it out of the way and around its shape. The efficiency with which a bullet passes through the air is known as ballistic coefficient (BC). Manufacturers determine the BC of their bullets and assign it a number. The higher the number, the higher the efficiency. Bullets with higher BCs, when compared with bullets of the same velocity with lower BCs, will have flatter trajectories. To complicate matters a little, the same bullet can have different BCs at different velocities. For example, a 190-grain BTHP Match King has a BC of .575 at 2,600 fps, and a BC of .530 at 1,700 fps.

Bullet-Cartridge Selection

Do not base your cartridge/bullet selection solely on BC. Once you have narrowed your bullet selection to those with acceptable accuracy and terminal performance, select those with the best trajectory and wind drift resistance for the distances you expect to encounter. Plugging possible bullet selections into a computer program, along with obtainable velocities, will reveal the best bullet-cartridge combinations. Depending on your intended use range, the bullet with the highest BC may not be the best choice. For example, your intended use range is 0 to 1,000 yards, the cartridge is .300 WM, and the bullet selection, based mainly on accuracy, is the

Sierra Match King. The .30-caliber Sierra Match King bullet weights start at 150 grains, with a BC of .456. The bullet's progression in weight and BC is as follows:

Bullet Weight	Ballistic Coefficient
155	.470
168	.475
180	.514
190	.575
200	.600
220	.655
250	.697

30 CAL MK

GRN	BC	VELOCITY	1000 YD DROP—IN	1000 YD DRIFT—IN
150	.456	3300	223	63
168	.475	3200	233	63
180	.514	3100	241	59
190	.575	3000	245	54
200	.600	2900	260	54
220	.655	2750	282	52
250	.697	2600	313	53

This chart illustrates .30-caliber bullets fired at moderate magnum velocities. Note how the bullet weight and BC go up, while the velocity goes down. As the velocity drops, so does the bullet's impact at 1,000 yards. The wind drift resistance slightly favors the heavier bullet at 1,000 yards, until the weight gets too high and the velocity too low. Ballistic computers save the shooter several steps in load development.

Remember, you are working within the parameters of the .300 WM cartridge, and as the bullet weight and BC increase, the obtainable muzzle velocity decreases. By comparing ballistic charts, you can see that at the maximum intended-use range of 1,000 yards, the lighter bullet at a higher velocity has a substantially flatter trajectory, while almost equaling the wind drift resistance of the heavier bullets. The higher BC of the heavier bullet shows advantages at extreme ranges, but these are well beyond the 0-to-1,000-yard expected-use ranges. Even though the BC is less, the lighter bullet may be the better selection in this example, provided that the lighter bullet meets your other performance requirements. Keep in mind that computer-generated ballistic charts are only unproven overviews of ballistic performance. All bullet-load combinations must be thoroughly range tested prior to adoption. Experience has shown that commonly twisted .300 WM rifles perform better with bullets in the 190-to-200-grain range.

Your rifle barrel has to have the correct twist rate to fire the selected bullet accurately; a better trajectory will mean little if the bullet is not accurate. Consider the big picture when selecting your bullet-cartridge-rifle combination.

Bullet shapes have a direct effect on a bullet's BC rating. Blunt-nose and flat-base bullets have less flight efficiency than streamlined BT designs. Bullets that have only a slight difference in BC will have only a small difference in trajectory at ranges less than 500 yards. Extended-range trajectories show benefits in even small increases in BC, provided that the bullets are started at the same velocity. Bullets with different BCs, fired at varying velocities, need their expected-use ranges defined to determine what will best meet the requirements. Evaluation of

The following charts are a rough guideline for the .300 WM at 4,500 feet. An example of what to look for can be seen when comparing the lightest to the heaviest bullets listed. A 155-grain BTHP bullet with a BC of .475 and a muzzle velocity of 3,300 fps will drop 34.7 inches at 500 yards from its 100-yard zero and drift 12.9 inches in a 10-mph crosswind. At 1,000 yards, the same bullet drops 217.6 inches and drifts 60.4 inches. The 250-grain BTHP with a much higher BC of .697 but a lower MV of 2,600 fps will drop 55 inches at 500 yards and drift 12.5 inches. At 1,000 yards the same bullet will drop 313.3 inches and drift 53.3 inches. The 250-grain bullet thus has a slight drift resistance edge, while the light bullet has a substantial edge in its ability to shoot flatter. All-around best field performance in standard twisted .300 WM rifles has been with bullets in the 190-to-200-grain range.

150 GRN, 30 CAL

```
4500 FEET            59 DEG. F
BC: .456  CORRECTED: .539
VELOCITY: 3300.0 FPS
SIGHT HEIGHT:              1.5
CROSS WIND:          10 MPH
ZERO RANGE:               100
        +0.0 @ 100 YARDS
```

DIST	PATH	DRIFT
100	+0.0	0.4
200	−2.1	1.8
300	−8.3	4.6
400	−19.0	8.1
500	−35.3	13.7
600	−57.2	20.4
700	−85.9	28.5
800	−122.2	38.2
900	−167.6	63.7
1000	−223.0	63.7

155 GRN, 30 CAL

```
4500 FEET            59 DEG. F
BC: .475  CORRECTED: .562
VELOCITY: 3300.0 FPS
SIGHT HEIGHT:              1.5
CROSS WIND:          10 MPH
ZERO RANGE:               100
        +0.0 @ 100 YARDS
```

DIST	PATH	DRIFT
100	+0.0	0.4
200	−2.1	1.8
300	−8.2	4.2
400	−18.9	7.9
500	−34.7	12.9
600	−56.5	19.5
700	−84.5	27.1
800	−119.8	36.3
900	−163.6	47.2
1000	−217.6	60.4

168 GRN, 30 CAL

```
4500 FEET            59 DEG. F
BC: .475  CORRECTED: .562
VELOCITY: 3200.0 FPS
SIGHT HEIGHT:              1.5
CROSS WIND:          10 MPH
ZERO RANGE:               100
        +0.0 @ 100 YARDS
```

DIST	PATH	DRIFT
100	+0.0	0.5
200	−2.3	1.8
300	−8.9	4.6
400	−20.3	8.3
500	−37.4	13.7
600	−60.6	20.2
700	−90.7	28.3
800	−128.8	38.0
900	−175.8	49.5
1000	−233.5	63.0

180 GRN, 30 CAL

```
4500 FEET            59 DEG. F
BC: .514  CORRECTED: .608
VELOCITY: 3100.0 FPS
SIGHT HEIGHT:              1.5
CROSS WIND:          10 MPH
ZERO RANGE:               100
        +0.0 @ 100 YARDS
```

DIST	PATH	DRIFT
100	+0.0	0.2
200	−2.6	1.8
300	−9.6	4.2
400	−21.7	7.9
500	−39.8	13.2
600	−63.9	19.4
700	−95.1	27.1
800	−134.1	36.1
900	−182.5	47.0
1000	−241.0	59.7

190 GRN, 30 CAL

```
4500 FEET            59 DEG. F
BC: .575  CORRECTED: .680
VELOCITY: 3000.0 FPS
SIGHT HEIGHT:              1.5
CROSS WIND:          10 MPH
ZERO RANGE:               100
        +0.0 @ 100 YARDS
```

DIST	PATH	DRIFT
100	+0.0	0.4
200	−2.7	1.6
300	−10.2	3.9
400	−23.0	7.6
500	−41.7	12.3
600	−66.6	18.0
700	−98.2	24.6
800	−138.0	32.9
900	−186.7	42.8
1000	−245.3	54.2

200 GRN, 30 CAL

```
4500 FEET            59 DEG. F
BC: .600  CORRECTED: .710
VELOCITY: 2900.0 FPS
SIGHT HEIGHT:              1.5
CROSS WIND:          10 MPH
ZERO RANGE:               100
        +0.0 @ 100 YARDS
```

DIST	PATH	DRIFT
100	+0.0	0.7
200	−3.0	1.8
300	−11.0	4.0
400	−24.9	7.9
500	−44.6	12.5
600	−70.8	17.8
700	−105.0	25.0
800	−146.8	32.9
900	−198.1	42.8
1000	−260.0	54.4

220 GRN, 30 CAL

4500 FEET   59 DEG. F
BC: .655   CORRECTED: .775
VELOCITY: 2750.0 FPS
SIGHT HEIGHT: 1.5
CROSS WIND: 10 MPH
ZERO RANGE: 100
     +0.0 @ 100 YARDS

DIST	PATH	DRIFT
100	+0.0	0.4
200	−3.5	1.6
300	−12.9	4.6
400	−28.0	7.9
500	−49.8	12.3
600	−78.8	17.6
700	−115.7	24.3
800	−161.2	32.2
900	−216.7	41.7
1000	−282.7	52.6

250 GRN, 30 CAL

4500 FEET   59 DEG. F
BC: .697   CORRECTED: .824
VELOCITY: 2600.0 FPS
SIGHT HEIGHT: 1.5
CROSS WIND: 10 MPH
ZERO RANGE: 100
     +0.0 @ 100 YARDS

DIST	PATH	DRIFT
100	+0.0	0.5
200	−4.3	2.5
300	−14.6	4.8
400	−31.6	7.9
500	−55.9	12.5
600	−88.0	18.0
700	−129.0	24.6
800	−179.4	32.7
900	−240.6	42.4
1000	−313.3	53.3

250 GRN, 338 CAL

4500 FEET   59 DEG. F
BC: .587   CORRECTED: .694
VELOCITY: 3000.0 FPS
SIGHT HEIGHT: 1.5
CROSS WIND: 10 MPH
ZERO RANGE: 100
     +0.0 @ 100 YARDS

DIST	PATH	DRIFT
100	+0.0	0.2
200	−2.8	1.8
300	−10.2	3.9
400	−22.9	7.2
500	−41.6	12.0
600	−66.4	17.6
700	−98.1	24.3
800	−137.3	32.2
900	−185.4	41.7
1000	−243.5	53.0

750 GRN, 50 CAL SPITZER

BC: .820   VEL: 2550 FPS
SIGHT HEIGHT: 1.5
CROSS WIND: 10 MPH
ZERO RANGE: 100
     +0.0 @ 100 YARDS

DIST	PATH	DRIFT	VELOCITY
500	−51.2	11.6	2178.8
1000	−288.4	50.7	1720.8
1500	−821.8	126.7	1345.2
2000	−1814.1	248.7	1092.7
2500	−3416.0	411.1	956.4

155 GRN, 300 WM PALMA

BC: .475   VEL: 3400 FPS
SIGHT HEIGHT: 1.5
CROSS WIND: 10 MPH
ZERO RANGE: 100
     +0.0 @ 100 YARDS

DIST	PATH	DRIFT	VELOCITY
500	−32.8	14.8	2440.3
1000	−218.3	70.9	1634.3
1500	−734.7	194.5	1104.2
2000	−1823.4	387.5	894.1
2500	−3672.0	630.8	771.2

168 GRN, 308 WIN BTHP

BC: .475   VEL: 2550 FPS
SIGHT HEIGHT: 1.5
CROSS WIND: 10 MPH
ZERO RANGE: 100
     +0.0 @ 100 YARDS

DIST	PATH	DRIFT	VELOCITY
500	−67.6	23.4	1720.1
1000	−440.3	110.6	1146.7
1500	−1384.1	269.5	912.6
2000	−3114.9	480.1	784.1
2500	−5872.0	738.1	685.0

STUB-BARREL 308 WIN COMPARED TO LR 300 WIN MAG

308 WIN				300 WIN MAG		

4500 FEET · 70 DEG. F
BC: .475 · CORRECTED: .574
VELOCITY: 2500.0 FPS
SIGHT HEIGHT: 1.5
CROSS WIND: 10 MPH
ZERO RANGE: 100
+0.0 @ 100 YARDS

4500 FEET · 70 DEG. F
BC: .475 · CORRECTED: .574
VELOCITY: 3300.0 FPS
SIGHT HEIGHT: 1.5
CROSS WIND: 10 MPH
ZERO RANGE: 100
+0.0 @ 100 YARDS

DIST	PATH	DRIFT		DIST	PATH	DRIFT
50	+0.0	0.5		50	−0.3	0.2
100	+0.0	1.2		100	+0.0	0.4
150	−1.6	2.1		150	−0.6	1.1
200	−4.8	3.2		200	−2.0	1.6
250	−9.8	4.8		250	−4.6	2.8
300	−16.7	6.9		300	−8.2	4.2
350	−25.6	9.2		350	−12.8	5.8
400	−36.8	12.1		400	−18.7	7.6
450	−50.1	15.3		450	−25.8	9.9
500	−66.1	19.2		500	−34.4	12.5
550	−84.8	23.6		550	−44.5	15.7
600	−106.3	28.5		600	−56.0	19.0
650	−130.7	33.8		650	−68.9	22.4
700	−158.4	39.8		700	−83.7	26.4
750	−189.6	46.3		750	−100.3	30.6
800	−224.9	53.7		800	−118.8	35.4
850	−263.4	61.3		850	−139.4	40.5
900	−306.5	69.7		900	−162.2	46.1
950	−354.2	78.9		950	−187.1	51.9
1000	−406.8	88.7		1000	−214.9	58.6

Reviewing these long-range ballistic charts will show why extreme-range shooters select bullets with high-ballistic coefficients. The .50-caliber, 750-grain bullet with a BC of .820 surpasses the higher velocity magnum cartridge's bullet with a BC of .475 at extreme range trajectory and has superior wind-drift resistance at all ranges. Trajectory is predictable, wind drift is variable, and so wind-drift resistance is a very important factor. The .308 Winchester lags far behind the .300 WM and .50-caliber in extended-range ballistics. In situations where energy and penetration are important, the .50-caliber has a substantial advantage. The 750-grain bullet has more energy at 1 mile than the .308 has at the muzzle— not to mention that an armor-piercing bullet of .50 caliber will punch through more than 1.5 inches of steel at 100 yards.

The majority of police marksman situations simply won't require a cartridge as powerful as the .50-caliber, but it could prove very valuable in specialized missions. The 1993 cult standoff in Waco, Texas, certainly demonstrated how the police may have to face such a weapon in civilian law enforcement.

220 GRN, 30 CAL WILDCAT

4500 FEET		80 DEG. F
BC: .640	CORRECTED: .778	
VELOCITY: 3115.0 FPS		
SIGHT HEIGHT:		1.5
CROSS WIND:		10 MPH
ZERO RANGE:		100

+0.0 @ 100 YARDS

DIST	PATH	DRIFT
100	+0.0	0.5
200	−2.4	1.4
300	−9.0	3.3
400	−20.1	5.8
500	−36.3	9.3
600	−58.5	14.4
700	−86.4	20.1
800	−120.7	26.6
900	−162.2	34.2
1000	−211.2	42.8

180 GRN, 30 CAL WILDCAT

4500 FEET		80 DEG. F
BC: .498	CORRECTED: .613	
VELOCITY: 3600.0 FPS		
SIGHT HEIGHT:		1.5
CROSS WIND:		10 MPH
ZERO RANGE:		100

+0.0 @ 100 YARDS

DIST	PATH	DRIFT
100	+0.0	0.7
200	−1.5	1.8
300	−6.3	3.9
400	−14.6	6.7
500	−27.3	10.7
600	−44.1	15.5
700	−66.4	21.8
800	−94.5	29.4
900	−128.4	37.8
1000	−169.8	48.1

45 ACP/22—250

45 ACP CARBINE
230 GRN ROUND NOSE

4500 FEET		80 DEG. F
BC: .160	CORRECTED: .197	
VELOCITY: 950.0 FPS		
SIGHT HEIGHT:		1.5
CROSS WIND:		10 MPH
ZERO RANGE:		50

−9.1 @ 100 YARDS

DIST	PATH	DRIFT
50	+0.0	0.7
100	−9.1	2.8
150	−29.3	5.5
200	−61.8	9.7
250	−107.3	15.1

22—250 VARMIT CARTRIDGE
52 GRN HPBT

4500 FEET		80 DEG. F
BC: .232	CORRECTED: .286	
VELOCITY: 3700.0 FPS		
SIGHT HEIGHT:		1.5
CROSS WIND:		10 MPH
ZERO RANGE:		100

+0.0 @ 100 YARDS

DIST	PATH	DRIFT
100	+0.0	0.9
200	−1.7	3.5
300	−7.3	8.1
400	−18.2	15.5
500	−35.2	25.3
600	−60.5	38.6
700	−96.4	55.6
800	−146.4	77.8
900	−214.3	105.4
1000	−303.5	138.2

cartridges and ballistic charts may lead the shooter to select high-velocity bullets with a medium BC for use at moderate distances. Extreme-range cartridge evaluation will lead the shooter into heavier bullets with higher BCs. (See the accompanying BC-velocity comparison charts.)

Trajectory

Once the selection of a rifle-scope and cartridge-bullet combination is complete, you must understand the system's trajectory and the fact that the trajectory will change if any of the components are changed.

The system will have a trajectory of its own, based on the components used and the zero procedure you apply. For example, a .308 Winchester with 168-grain BTHP bullets at a velocity of 2,600 fps zeroed at 100 yards will cross your line of sight twice. The firearm has to be angled up in order to compensate for gravity, and the upward angle of the bullet's departure from the muzzle will have to be sufficient to allow the bullet to arc into the 100-yard zero point. The bullet will pass the line of sight near the muzzle and a second time at the zero point. In the case of the .308 Winchester, it will pass the line of sight (located 1.5 inches above the bore) at approximately 50 yards. The bullet will travel slightly above the line of sight before intersecting with the zero point and line of sight again at 100 yards.

From left to right: .223, .308 Winchester, .300 WM, and .50-caliber, 750-grain bullet.

The same cartridge zeroed for 200 yards would arc through the line of sight near the muzzle, remain over the line of sight by more than 2 inches at the 100-yard mark and make its second intersection with the line of sight at 200 yards.

Zeroing at extended ranges requires that the angle of bullet departure be more severe, which will result in a substantial high point (over the sightline) in the bullet's trajectory. For example, a .308 Winchester with a muzzle velocity of 2,500 fps, zeroed at 500 yards, will arc approximately 24 inches over the sightline at approximately 300 yards and drop approximately 318 inches below the sightline by the time it reaches 1,000 yards. This can lead to bullet impact on obstructions that the shooter may not have considered. An example is a marksman shooting at a distant target under midrange tree limbs. The sight picture on target may be perfectly clear, but if the shooter does not consider midrange trajectory, the bullet may be deflected by the tree limbs. Such obstructions as power lines, fences, and doorways must be considered when calculating a shot. (Effective zeroing procedures are covered in Chapter 6.)

Once you learn the trajectory of the system you are shooting, you will need to know the distance to the target. Without this knowledge, you cannot determine the proper hold or dial-in information. Because you know that the bullet's flight is not straight, in contrast to the line of sight, you also know that causing your bullet to hit the target requires much more than basic marksmanship skills. Learning how far the bullet is from the line of sight at different ranges, and how to compensate for this, is not difficult; it is simply a matter of rigorous training. Remember, single-shot hits under unknown conditions in stressful situations are the circumstances under which the tactical marksman is expected to perform.

Other influences on bullet flight must be considered when the shot is being calculated. Wind drift (deflection) is one of the most important because wind will deflect a bullet in flight, thereby causing a bullet's impact to be off the mark if there is no compensation for the drift in advance of the shot. Wind deflection is, of course, greatest when the wind is blowing roughly horizontal at a 90-degree angle to the bullet's flight (a 90-degree crosswind). Wind at the same velocity but at different angles to the bullet's flight will have less "value," or less influence, on the bullet's flight. Common field terms for expressing wind-deflection value are *full value, half value*, and *no value*. Full value is 90-degree wind, half value is 45-degree wind, and no value wind is head wind or tail wind. No-value winds add velocity or air resistance, but the increased or decreased vertical bullet placement (unless extreme) will not be readily noticed at less than 500 yards.

You must figure wind into your shot calculation by its value, and predetermining the wind drift of your individual cartridge/load is a step in the right direction. Wind drift should be figured on a 90-degree, 10-mph crosswind basis out to the maximum distance you are responsible for shooting. From this information in your field data book, you can make your wind compensations. As an example, your information may indicate that your bullet will drift 5 inches at 200 yards in a 90-degree, 10-mph crosswind. In the field when you are faced with a 200-yard shot with a 20-mph crosswind, simply double the amount of drift compensation to 10 inches.

In another example, assume the same data at 200 yards. You are faced with a 200-yard shot with a 45-degree (or half-value) wind of 10 mph. Reduce your drift compensation to 2.5 inches.

Shooters equipped with accurate wind meters may want to figure the drift information of their bullet at a 1-mph crosswind. They then simply take the amount of determined bullet drift and multiply it by the amount of wind to determine compensation.

For example, at 200 yards a 1-mph wind will drift your bullet 1 inch. Your wind meter indicates a 5-mph crosswind; therefore, 5 inches is required for drift compensation. (Note that these are simplified examples of crosswind calculations and compensations. They are not meant to follow any particular wind drift data.)

Shooters not equipped with portable wind meters will have to judge wind by observing the effects it has on their surroundings. Flags, smoke, leaves, trash, grass, trees, and dust give the shooter an idea of both wind direction and velocity. Rain and snowfall can also be used as wind speed and direction indicators, but keep in mind that your bullet will have to pass through these conditions if a shot is required. Position yourself as close to the target as possible, or wait for a lull to minimize its effects—do not let water build up in your bore before the shot, or accuracy may be adversely affected.

As stated earlier, the wind at the shooting position may be substantially different than where the target is located—not to mention what it might be in intervening areas. Making a bullet travel through sheltered and nonsheltered areas, turbulence, and variable conditions will make the calculations more difficult. Intensive training and experience are required for accurate performance. Choosing a bullet-cartridge combination with the best practical trajectory and wind resistance will minimize the errors caused by wind drift and rainbow trajectories. Select your firing position, whenever possible, to negate crosswinds.

Temperature

Temperature is another influence on a bullet's performance. Warmer ammunition increases its pressure and velocity. Higher air temperatures mean less air density and less drag on the bullet's flight, which equates to higher POI. Keep in mind that ammunition loaded near maximum pressures in cool temperatures can generate dangerous pressures when fired at hot temperatures; this needs to be taken into account during load development. Conversely, lower temperatures mean lower velocity and POI because colder air is denser and puts more drag on the bullet. A rifle zeroed in winter conditions and fired in summer conditions will shoot high.

In my experience, these POI changes have been most noticeable in the middle temperatures, with smaller impact changes during variations in either the extreme highs or lows. Practice and notations need to be made in your own environment, with your own equipment and ammunition, to determine the required compensation. A 15-to-20-degree temperature change will normally require compensation for impact change. New products are currently being developed and tested that will reportedly negate ammunition pressure changes that result from temperature. Once perfected, these powders will make the marksman's job a little easier.

A top-quality portable temperature/humidity meter is a helpful asset when determining necessary compensation. As a tactical marksman, you should keep your rifle zeroed as close as possible to the existing environmental conditions in his area. Anytime you have an opportunity to confirm the zero on the way to a situation, do it.

Geographical Elevation

Shooting at higher elevations also affects bullet performance. Higher elevation means higher POI because the air there has less density, thus less drag on the bullet. Elevation changes of 1,000 feet require zero confirmation and, possibly, compensation. Here, again, you have to develop logbook data for your own equipment in order to determine accurate compensations.

Air Density and Humidity

Air density (i.e., barometric pressure) and humidity can also affect bullet flight. More air density equals more drag and lower POI. Log the barometric pressure for your area and the effect it may have on the zero of your rifle to determine what corrections must be made (normally, a change of 1 inch of mercury or more requires compensation to remain precisely zeroed). Also monitor humidity: high humidity means higher drag and lower POI. Monitor changes in humidity and their effects on your zero to determine suitable compensation. Again, record detailed data and make data book entries for field use.

Angles

Angle shooting can have a substantial effect on POI and seems to be misunderstood by many shooters. Angle shooting can be easily understood by realizing that gravity only acts on a projectile (your bullet) during the distance it travels on the horizontal line. For example, you are on the ground shooting up at a rooftop sniper. The direct distance to the target is 300 yards. The upward angle is 40 degrees. To determine your sight setting, take 300 x .77 and figure your sight setting to be for 231 yards. Calculate the wind drift for the entire 300 yards. Address other environmental factors and make the shot. The multiplication factor changes, of course, when calculating different angles.

Rule of thumb: Estimate the on-the-level-distance to your target and use that distance in your trajectory determination. Estimate the angled direct distance to the target and use that distance to determine wind drift. Angle shooting is a vital skill for the tactical marksman; shooting down from an observation point, or up at a rooftop sniper, could easily be a requirement of the position. The details of angle shooting are covered in detail during countersniper training courses.

There are many things to be considered when calculating the shot. Making a difficult shot will require thorough knowledge, proper training, and equipment. Whenever practical, choose a position or hide that reduces angles, wind drift, and distance, while still providing acceptable cover, concealment, and avenue of escape. In-depth study of external factors and an understanding of marksmanship, ballistics, fieldcraft, and countersniper tactics will best enable you to select positions.

TERMINAL BALLISTICS

Terminal ballistics is the study of a bullet's impact performance on a target. Terminal performance is the result achieved from the target being hit by the bullet. When the police marksman has to shoot a hostile target to save innocent people from death or serious bodily injury, the hostile target will often be in close proximity to innocent people. In such a situation, instant, no-reflex incapacitation is the goal of the police marksman—anything short of this can result in injury to innocent people.

A central nervous system (CNS) hit is the surest way to achieve no-reflex incapacitation, but even that may not always ensure that no *involuntary reflex action* or resultant harmful event occurs after the shot. Any movement of a hostile target's body parts or spasm may be enough to set off an explosive device or discharge a firearm. Therefore, the police marksman must be aware of the hostile's hand positions at the time of the shot to avoid undesired occurrences. If the CNS is not immediately destroyed, the hostile's shutdown is more unpredictable; the hostile's body may continue to function after a deadly body shot for about 15 seconds, or until blood pressure drops and the brain's oxygen supply is gone. (Game hunters often experience situations where a high-powered rifle shot has completely blown the heart out of an animal, yet it continues to bolt a substantial distance before dropping.)

The best way to describe the immediate reaction to non-CNS hits is "substantially uncertain." Different people are affected in different ways, because of many factors. The mind-set or determination of the hostile may have a substantial effect on his actions after receiving non-CNS hits. The human will to fight, live, or flee varies from person to person. Human determination to complete an act, even though mortally wounded, can be an amazingly powerful force. Drugs and alcohol may also play an important role in whether the shot's effect is immediate or not. However, at the other extreme, some people are rendered functionless by only minor wounds: their preoccupation with a wound may be so great that they lose sight of their surroundings or original intentions.

Precise shot placement is required to ensure CNS hits. This, of course, requires accurate equipment and diligent training. Sufficient training time greatly outweighs actual call-out time. This can be a hard bill for law enforcement administrators to pay, but it is the only way to maximize the probability of success.

Not every situation permits optimal shot placement for shutting down the CNS. Obstacles may include hard cover, the presence of innocent bystanders or hostages, or an unacceptable backstop. In these cases, the marksman may be forced to take a center mass shot on the available target. The results achieved from a center shot depend not only on the individual, but also on what is hit and the type of wound inflicted.

Ammunition

To increase the chances of a non-CNS shot instantly incapacitating the target, you must select the proper bullets. There is yet no final word on this subject. The ammunition used by marksmen must perform well in multiple areas. It must fly well, be accurate, have correct penetration without unpredictable fragmentation, and have proper terminal effect on the target.

The tactical marksman can make use of the competition shooters' study and evaluation of accurate bullets and quest for top performance from their firearms, ammunition, and scopes. For instance, as of this writing, the match BTHP bullet is generally accepted as the most consistently accurate choice in bullet design for the long-range rifleman.

The tactical marksman should take into consideration that the match BTHP bullet is designed with accuracy as its first priority, featuring aerodynamic shape and balance that, combined with tight quality control of weight and concentricity, lead to consistently accurate bullets. The BTHP match bullet is not designed for penetration without fragmentation, nor for terminal performance. The hollow point of the match bullet is not designed for expansion; it is simply a product of the manufacturing process.

Match bullets at high velocity may deliver good terminal performance on torso shots as a result of shock and fragmentation, or they may provide minimal terminal performance by acting similarly to some full-metal jacket (FMJ) bullets. The BTHP, especially at longer ranges and lower velocities, can pass through a target without any deformation and with little effect.

Remember that glass penetration with BTHP match bullets is also inconsistent (glass thickness and angle of the shot are, of course, factors in deflection and fragmentation). In my tests, BTHP bullets fired at close to medium range, at .308 Winchester velocities, have had inconsistent effects on glass. Bullet fragmentation and deflection are the most common types of failure of the match bullet. Introduction of the Federal .308 tactical load has greatly improved penetration performance.

The tactical marksman required to fire through barriers needs four things from his bullet: accuracy, penetration without fragmentation, terminal effect, and high ballistic efficiency. Numerous custom bullet makers offer bullets possessing one or two of these criteria (e.g., penetration with excellent weight retention and terminal performance). The same bullet may be lacking in other areas critical to the tactical marksman (e.g, accuracy, ballistic efficiency). Knowledgeable bullet makers have addressed this concern for their big-game hunting clientele. The custom bullet offers accuracy, penetration without fragmentation, terminal performance, and an aerodynamic boat-tailed (BT) design for high ballistic efficiency.

The manufacturer accomplishes this by individually turning concentric solid BT bullets, bonding a lead core in the front portion of the bullet, and capping it with a pointed nylon tip. This yields good accuracy, an aerodynamic shape, lead tip performance without deformation, and penetration without common jacket-core separation. The bonded-core custom bullets perform well; the drawback is

The two targets in these photos illustrate match bullet fragmentation after glass penetration. The cartridge used was Federal .308 Winchester Match 168-grain BTHP at approximately 2,550 fps.

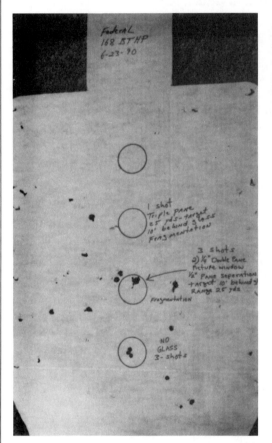
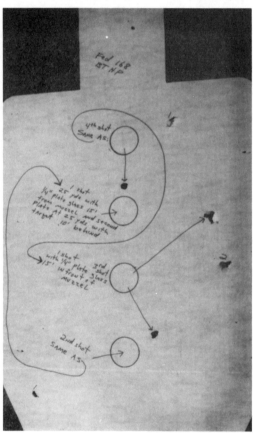

their cost. At $2 to $3 per bullet, most shooters will not be able to practice with them as much as needed, and training is mandatory for proper performance. If you select a custom bullet, be sure your budget can support adequate training with it.

The solid-copper hollow point bullet that has gained a good hunting reputation for terminal performance and penetration without fragmentation. This bullet is manufactured in larger lots than custom bullets, so, although it is more expensive than most mass-produced bullets, it is not nearly as expensive as a true custom bullet. My experience with the solid-copper hollow point bullet has yielded less than match accuracy performance.

Federal has introduced a 165-grain, bonded-core "tactical load." The soft point and bonded core enhance terminal performance and penetration without fragmentation.

My initial testing with the Federal .308 TL indicates that it is capable of sub-1.5 MOA. The trajectory is very similar to the Federal .308 Match load out to 200 yards. After serious range testing, it may fit some of the special requirements of .308 tactical shooters.

Bullet development seems to be headed in the right direction to meet the tactical marksman's requirements, but a clear, cost-effective single bullet winner is not available as of this writing. The Sierra Match King seems to be the accepted standard and performs extremely well in the accuracy category. Federal's Match .308 loading with this bullet has been a proven accuracy performer for many years.

Remember to evaluate bullet accuracy at maximum expected range, as well as at close range. Some bullets print well at close range, but don't maintain consistency at longer distances. Don't undercut your rifle's accuracy by selecting an inferior bullet. Nonconcentric bullets can easily open up the groups of a 1/4-inch rifle to that of a multi-inch pattern. High-quality bullets are an important factor in obtaining optimum accuracy.

Shooters should evaluate the ballistic performance of bullets thoroughly because once a load is selected, much work will go into building a data book based on the cartridge's performance. This data will only be suitable for the specific bullet-load-rifle-scope combination with which it was developed. Choosing the correct combination the first time will prevent you from having to duplicate your efforts. A ballistic computer program helps you to narrow the field of bullets from which to choose, but everything must be range tested.

As bullet weight and BC increase, muzzle velocity will decrease in a given cartridge. Make the best selection for your needs. The chart on page 85 provides a rough guideline for the .300 Winchester Magnum, with elevation at 4,500 feet. An example of what to look for can be seen when comparing the lightest to the heaviest bullets listed. A 155-grain BTHP bullet with a BC of .475 and a muzzle velocity of 3,300 fps will drop 34.7 inches at 500 yards from its 100-yard zero

Premium bullets are a must for the marksman.

and drift 12.9 inches in a 10-mph crosswind. At 1,000 yards, the same bullet drops 217.6 inches and drifts 60.4 inches. The 250-grain BTHP with a much higher BC of .697 but a lower muzzle velocity of 2,600 fps will drop 55 inches at 500 yards and drift 12.5 inches. At 1,000 yards, the same bullet will drop 313.3 inches and drift 53.3 inches. The drift resistance edge is only slightly in favor of the 250-grain bullet, while the light bullet holds a substantial edge with its ability to shoot flatter. A shooter wanting to engage unarmored targets in the 0-to-1,000-yard range and having only basic range-finding equipment may want to opt for the flatter shooting bullet. A shooter requiring more penetration and energy on impact, and having access to accurate range-finding equipment, may opt for the heavy bullet loading. Accurate range-finding equipment may allow the shooter to put less emphasis on a flat shooting load and use the added wind drift resistance of the heavier bullet.

The bullet is only a part of your ammunition selection. Cartridge components and assembly procedures could be a book in itself. Many tactical marksmen will find themselves limited by departmental regulation to commonly accepted factory-loaded ammunition. Even though ammunition suited to an individual rifle performs better than factory ammo, this is a wise decision by a department making ammo regulations for the general officer. The problems arise when the department's inexperienced officers attempt to load ammunition. Now that ammunition factories are addressing the needs of the tactical marksman it would be wise to avoid the liability of handloads for tactical use.

Factory match ammunition will be far superior to any attempted by an inexperienced handloader. The professional marksman, even though a precision loader, will probably have to make do with factory match ammo. Past departmental experiences with poor-quality or dangerous ammunition, coupled with the liability issues tactical units face, may dictate that this regulation is inflexible. In that case, choose a rifle caliber such as .308 Winchester, where match ammo is available in factory loadings. Out of a properly accurized rifle they will achieve fine accuracy.

If you choose a factory cartridge without an available match loading, be sure to select the best performing, highest quality round. This would normally be one from a reputable company's premium line. For initial ammunition testing, obtain a sample of all premium ammunition brands and test-fire for accuracy. Narrow the field of possible choices based on accuracy from your individual rifle. Determine what bullet types are used in the factory ammunition and determine the bullet's ballistic coefficient and velocity to generate a computer ballistic chart. Check the ammunition for consistency over a quality chronograph, paying special attention to the velocity variation in a string of shots. A very small velocity deviation over an entire string of shots indicates consistency in the ammunition.

Disassemble a sampling of cartridges and weigh the individual components. Check the consistency of bullet, case, and powder charge weights, and get an overall, average cartridge weight. All duty cartridges should be individually weighed and compared to the average weight determined by your sampling. Any cartridge whose weight indicates that it is substantially lighter or heavier than the average should not be used for duty. The weight check should be done on an accurate electronic scale that can be calibrated before each use. A bullet, case, and overall

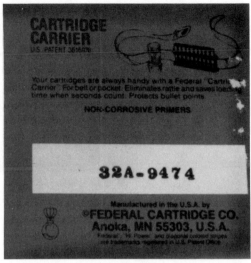

cartridge concentricity check should be made with the correct benchrest equipment to further evaluate ammunition. The bottom line on factory ammunition is that if you did not personally assemble the cartridge, you don't know what it contains; you are depending on someone else's quality standards. Periodic factory recalls of ammunition because of assembly mistakes should be enough incentive to make you narrow the potential for problems by checking cartridge weights; but even this won't detect a primer without an anvil or a case without a flash hole. If you shoot factory ammunition, use only the most reputable, reliable, accurate ammunition available, and double-check it. Buy ammunition in large quantities and always of the same lot number.

Handloaded Ammunition

The true precision handloader is capable of tailoring ammunition to individual rifles so that it will outperform factory ammunition in accuracy and performance. Precision loading techniques have been repeatedly proven in benchrest accuracy competition. Some of these techniques are applicable to ammunition suitable for the field marksman; others aren't. Achieving the best performance possible without adversely affecting reliability is a priority. For example, one benchrest shooter/precision loader may determine that light neck tension and a bullet seated into the lands give an additional 1/10-inch off his 100-yard group. Ammunition loaded in this manner may require that the shooter fire it after it is chambered or face the probability of the bullet remaining stuck in the lands when the cartridge is not fired and the bolt is opened. Pulling the unfired bulletless case out of the chamber, of course, results in fine powder granules being spilled in the action. Of course, this is unsuitable for the tactical marksman who will, more often than not, complete his mission without firing at all. Any ammunition assembled for the tactical marksman must be loaded for precision, but with reliability as priority one.

Federal .308 Winchester Match ammunition is currently the accepted standard in factory match ammunition. If you use precision handloads, they should be more consistent than the accepted standard. The charts on page 85 depict the

Handloading requires safety precautions. Don't take shortcuts with them.

(Right and below) A precision handloader has the opportunity to check every primer to make sure that an anvil is present and that every case has a flash hole.

loading and component consistency of five rounds of Federal Match .308 Winchester ammunition to five rounds of professionally loaded precision ammunition. Each five-round sample was taken from the same lot number of ammunition.

A brief overview of the steps necessary to assemble precision ammunition will explain why it may take more than 100 hours of intensive labor to assemble 500 rounds of precision ammunition. It is strictly a job for the perfectionist.

The ammunition being loaded should be suited to only one rifle. The chamber should be measured and the correct overall case length determined. The distance to the lands should be measured in order to determine correct overall loaded cartridge length. This length will have to be determined by where the rifle shoots most accurately (i.e., how far the bullet should be from the lands). Correct bullet, case, powder, and primer combinations will have to be determined for best performance. Cases will have to be fire-formed, uniformed, and checked for concentricity. Bullets, cases, and powder charges will all have to be individually weighed and painstakingly assembled to exacting dimensions. Loaded-round concentricity will have to be checked, and out-of-spec rounds discarded. Fired rounds will have to be checked for velocity and pressure signs. As the throat of the rifle barrel erodes, bullet-seating depth may need to be adjusted. When new or different lots of the same components are introduced to the loading procedure, the performance testing begins again.

In short, don't ask for something you are not willing to devote a lot of time and effort to. A friendly letter to Federal Cartridge Company requesting a match-grade .300 WM round may assist .300 WM shooters with ammunition acquisition.

The precision handloader has the opportunity to check every stage of the cartridge assembly process. Every component can be individually inspected for correctness—steps that are not cost-effective for mass ammunition manufacturers. Large ammunition producers putting in the "per box" time and effort of the precision handloader would probably have to charge more than $100 a box just for the time invested.

The precision handloader can verify the reliability of his components before assembly by inspecting for such items as complete flash holes and intact primer anvils, thus preventing misfires before they happen.

Using factory ammunition requires the shooter to rely on someone else's standards of inspection and uniformity—someone who may be more interested in getting off work at 5 o'clock than thinking about the tactical marksman who must use the ammunition.

I trust individually loaded ammunition only if I load it. Those taking the time to load properly will benefit from enhanced accuracy, a better match between bullet and the task at hand, and loadings with superior trajectories. All of this minimizes the chance of a miss.

Knowing what is in your ammunition generates confidence in your own and speculation about what is in other ammunition.

All complete cartridges, handloads or factory, should be weighed and

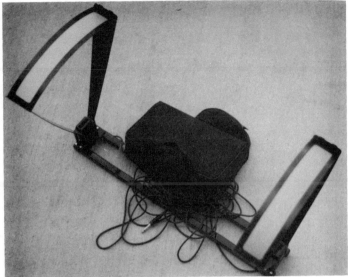

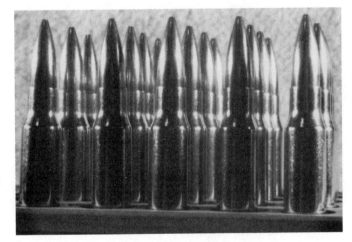

Accurate chronographing of your loads will provide valuable information on consistency. Ammo with larger velocity spreads will cause larger dispersion, especially at long ranges.

Precision handload development and assembly take knowledge and dedicated time. Properly done, they can outperform factory ammunition.

(Far left) Precision handloads should display detailed assembly data and be protected from contamination by a waterproof container.

(Left) All cartridges, whether factory or handloads, should be individually weighed prior to being placed in the "go" bag.

Precision ammunition comes from knowledgeable handloaders with precision tools.

Load development and testing is best accomplished with a high-powered target scope because it allows for a pinpoint hold and excellent accuracy evaluation. Shown here is a premier 18—40x custom scope.

gauged before duty carry. Non-gaugeable cartridges or cartridges with substantially different weights make the round unsuitable for duty carry.

A final note on ammo preparation: don't overestimate your abilities and experience. Use factory-prepared ammo if you have any doubts at all about your ability to prepare reliable precision loads.

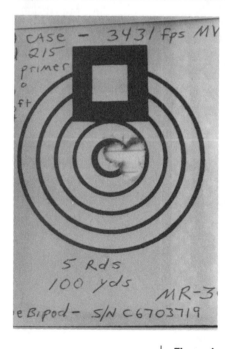
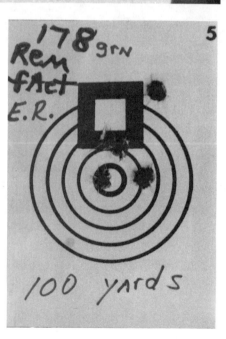
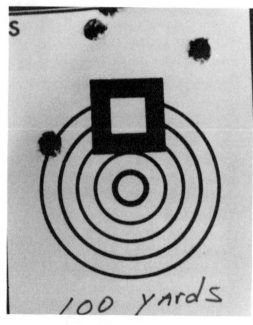

These shot groups were all fired on the same day by the same shooter from the same rifle at 100 yards. The right group was fired with nonconcentric bullets. The middle group was fired with factory ammo. The left group was fired with properly developed precision loads tailored to the individual rifle.

		RUNOUT OF BULLET IN LOADED CARTRIDGE	BULLET WEIGHT GRNS	POWDER CHARGE WEIGHT
FED MATCH 308	1	.005"	167	40.0
	2	.003"	168	39.8
	3	.005"	168	40.7
	4	.003"	168	40.5
	5	.005"	168	40.7
PRECISION LOADS	1	.001"	168	40.5
	2	.001"	168	40.5
	3	.001"	168	40.5
	4	.001"	168	40.5
	5	.001"	168	40.5

		CASE WEIGHTS	NECK THICKNESS	CASE LENGTH	PRIMER DEPTH
FED MATCH	1	164.7	.013	2.007	.003
	2	167.6	.014	2.008	.004
	3	163.7	.013	2.009	.003
	4	163.8	.015	2.009	.002
	5	165.7	.015	2.008	.003
PRECISION LOADS	1	164.2	.014	2.008	.003
	2	164.6	.014	2.008	.003
	3	164.5	.014	2.008	.003
	4	164.5	.014	2.008	.003
	5	164.4	.014	2.008	.003

Federal .308 Winchester Match ammunition is currently the accepted standard in factory match ammunition. The charts above depict the loading and component consistency of five rounds of Federal Match .308 Winchester to five rounds of professionally loaded ammunition. Each five-round sample was taken from the same lot #.

Extreme spread differences between Federal Match .308 Winchester and .300 WM precision loads.

EXTREME SPREAD DIFFERENCES BETWEEN FED MATCH 308 AND 300 WM PRECISION LOADS.

308 FED MATCH ES 66 FPS	300 WM PRECISION LOADS 24 FPS ES
2672	3415
2670	3410
2605	3434
2608	3411
2670	3414
2662	3425
2644	3431
2617	3429
2606	3426
2610	3430

Zeroing

ZEROING YOUR RIFLE IS A MATTER OF INTERSECTING YOUR BULLET AND LINE OF SIGHT at a specific point. The point at which you decide to make this intersection depends on your shooting requirements.

PRELIMINARY STEPS

Before you attempt the zeroing, be sure the scope is properly and securely mounted. If it is loose in the rings or mounts, your shot pattern will not be tight. If your equipment or personal shooting skills prevent you from shooting consistent groups, your developed data will not be accurate. If the scope is securely mounted, but you decide to change eye relief, ring height, or any other item that requires moving the scope, the zero will have to be reestablished after the adjustment is made. Top-quality scope bases and rings are essential for rigid scope mounting.

Mount the base of the scope securely to the rifle and then loosely attach the rings. More than two rings can be used for extra rigidity and scope protection. A straight, cylindrical steel bar of the same diameter as your scope tube should be placed in the rings and should be 1 inch in diameter for 1-inch scope tubes, and approximately 1 1/8 inch in diameter for 30mm tubes. The ring tops should be securely fastened over the bar to keep them in alignment on the base when the ring nuts are tightened and torqued. Remove the ring tops and hand lap the bottom portions of the rings into perfect alignment, thus permitting more surface area and friction to contact the scope tube and preventing kinking the scope tube when tightening it in place.

All threads should be completely degreased before final assembly. A thread-locking compound such as Loc-Tite #242 should be placed on the threads of the ring nuts before securing. The same should be done for the ring top screws before final installation. Do not use locking compounds that are designed to be permanent because scope damage may result during future disassembly.

The scope should rest on a friction compound in the ring to avoid slippage. Set the eye relief while it is in the most frequently used shooting position, and be sure the reticle is level with the rifle before alternating the tightening of the ring top screws. Once the scope and rifle are in vertical alignment, you must be sure not to cant the rifle during firing. A cant of only 1 degree will result in being 1/2 inch off at 100 yards, and 5 inches off at 1,000 yards. An anticant device (ACD) can be used to help the shooter keep the rifle level in the field.

The ammunition you use for zeroing should be the same as for duty use. Anytime ammunition lots are changed, you will need to rezero. Your ammunition should be kept together by lot numbers to avoid any confusion.

The shooting conditions for zeroing should be as close as possible to the geographic area to which you will be expected to respond. For zeroing or testing choose calm conditions; slow, undisturbed, deliberate, accurate shooting from a rest is called for when testing or zeroing. Less stable position shooting produces inaccurate information because there is too much human error factor involved in the results. If your groups do not correlate with the mechanical accuracy the rifle is capable of, correct your basic shooting skills. Do not adjust zero based on a poor shot pattern.

Zeroing should be accomplished from a solid rest only. Sandbags or a bipod works well. I recommend zeroing from your most stable, most commonly used field position.

TYPES OF ZEROING

There are two main types of zeroing: point-blank and specific range. The tactical marksman uses both.

Point-blank zeroing is choosing a zero point suited to the weapon system and the cartridge's trajectory that allows the shooter to hold the reticle centered on a target of specific size from point-blank range out to a specific distance. For example, if the target is 6 inches in diameter, you will want to determine a zero point that will not allow the bullet's trajectory to exceed 3 inches above or below the line of sight. The range where the bullet reaches 3 inches below the line of sight would be the maximum point-blank range. This range would be the farthest that a 6-inch target could be from the shooter and still receive a bullet impact with the reticle held on its center. The maximum point-blank range of a weapon system will vary according to the projectile's trajectory, the scope height, and the size of the intended target. The rifle launching the flattest shooting projectile will, of course, have the farthest point-blank range.

Specific-range, or specific-point, zeroing is simply choosing the exact range at which you want the bullet's path to intersect with your sightline. If you zero your rifle at 100 yards, for example, you will have to make any necessary compensations to achieve hits at other ranges.

Shooters going to the range with a new rifle-scope combination for the first time should use their collimators to bring their scope and bore into rough alignment. This saves time and ammunition once at the range. It should be stressed that collimator alignment of scope and bore does *not* constitute zeroing; it is only rough alignment. After completing initial zeroing, you can install the collimator and determine the remaining number of elevation and windage clicks. Compare the remaining elevation to the computer chart of your rifle's cartridge. If there is not enough elevation adjustment remaining in the scope to dial in a zero at the maximum range at which you intend to shoot, you can dismount the scope and make base adjustments to achieve the desired results. This is much more desirable than finding out near the end of the zeroing process that you didn't have quite enough clicks to achieve the maximum zero range desired.

The shooter using a new rifle, or newly rebarreled rifle, must break in the barrel to prolong its life. A special barrel break-in lubricant, such as a friction block, gives the best results. The ammunition fired in the barrel break-in process need not be wasted. It should be used to fine-tune the initial zero and as a rough test for accuracy.

Begin the process by swabbing the clean, new barrel with a patch lightly coated with Shooter's Choice or similar-quality solvent. Make sure you use a coated, one-piece cleaning rod and bore guide. Push the patch through and let it drop off the jag. Don't pull used patches back through the bore. Dry the bore with successive dry patches. Fire one round. Clean the barrel with solvent and a quality bronze core, bronze bristle brush (never stainless steel) on your coated cleaning rod. Make at least one complete pass with the brush, forward and back, for each round fired. Patch dry until clean. Fire two rounds and complete the same cleaning process. Fire three rounds and complete the same cleaning process. Continue this procedure for at least 20 rounds.

For the sake of limiting this chapter, I will assume that you will be using the two-rifle concept to cover close to extended ranges. The midrange carbine is intended for use at primarily close to medium ranges, probably less than 100 yards. The shooter needs to be able to overlap the midrange carbine's capability with the precision rifle in case exigencies arise. The same shooter should realize that he may be called off his post for close-range entry work. Close, fast action does not allow time for mechanical sight adjustments, so the point-blank zeroing procedure is best suited to the carbine.

The extended-range precision rifle is expected to provide precise bullet placement at all practical ranges. Calculate conditions and dial the zero into the correct range for best results. Provided that the precision rifle is equipped with the scope and data suitable for accomplishing this task, specific-range zeroing works best.

POINT-BLANK ZEROING

For the sake of simplicity, assume that you are issued a 5.56mm carbine with 55-grain ammunition. The bullets have a ballistic coefficient of .255. Corrected to your hypothetical geographical location, the BC is rated at .314. The muzzle velocity is 3,200 fps. The first attempt at point-blank zero is with an AR-15, with the scope mounted on the carrying handle and a sight height of 4.5 inches above the boreline. You are aware of your responsibility for accurate shot placement at close range and your need to overlap the carbine's performance with that of the precision bolt guns.

Not having access to a ballistic computer for sightline and trajectory calculations, you decide that a 50-yard zero may be sufficient for the relatively flat-shooting 5.56mm cartridge.

You set targets in 50-yard increments over the distance to be covered, point blank to 250 yards. Overlooking the difficulty of obtaining the correct cheek weld position with the high-scoped, straight-stocked weapon, you fire a slow, accurate group at 50 yards. A minor sight correction and another slow-fire group get you centered in the POA of the 50-yard target.

You have established the 50-yard zero point with your high-scoped AR-15. Your next task is to figure out how far you'll be able to shoot while aiming at the center of a 5-inch target.

Aiming at the center of the 5-inch target at point-blank range, such as during a room entry, you find that your bullets strike more than 4 inches low, well off the aiming point and the 5-inch target. You fire another group at the 50-yard target and find it to be centered in the POA. You have just confirmed that your point of zero is still correct. You now fire another slow-fire group at the center of the POA located at 100 yards. Checking the target indicates that you are well above the 5-inch circle, out of the acceptable hit area. Firing another slow-fire group at 150 yards, you find that your shot grouping is still consistent, but it is more than 6 inches above the POA. At 200 and 250 yards the shot groupings are well over 7 inches above the POA.

What you have is unacceptable zero performance at all ranges except very near the 50-yard area. You might think to yourself, *I thought the 5.56mm cartridge was a relatively flat shooter, so how can it be so far off the mark?*

The problem is sight height above the boreline. From Chapter 5, recall that the trajectory arc of the bullet must pass the line of sight on the way up and on the way down. The angle of departure of the bullet from the rifle allows the bullet to intersect with the sightline, which is located above the bore.

The carbine's performance will probably be required at close-to-medium ranges, so the zero was selected at 50 yards. For the bullet to reach the high sightline of the high-scoped AR-15 in such a short distance, the bullet must leave the rifle at a substantial upward angle. This angle will intersect the bullet and the sightline at 50 yards, but it will also carry the bullet high above the sightline before the bullet starts the downward portion of the arc.

This situation is totally unacceptable. The bullet must stay close enough to the line of sight to allow POA, POI on small-diameter targets from close-to-medium ranges without substantial compensations. Close action often means fast action. There is not time for mechanical sight adjustments or substantial thought about reticle-hold compensations.

There is an additional problem of high-mounting the scope on the AR-15. A high-scoped weapon requires the shooter to use the scope while clearing the muzzle from any cover object, thus exposing his upper body. Not uncommon are live-fire incidents during which a shooter will have a clear sight picture through the high scope, but the fired round hits the cover object at the end of the muzzle. This is dangerous not only because of fragmentation and position disclosure, but also because the shot normally misses the intended target. Increased neck strain from the elevated sighting position merely aggravates these problems.

These problems can be corrected, and a proper point-blank zero can be achieved

HIGH SCOPE/LOW SCOPE
AR 15 COMPARISON

LOW SCOPE 55 GRN, 224 CAL				HIGH SCOPE 55 GRN, 224 CAL		
4500 FEET	80 DEG. F			4500 FEET	80 DEG. F	
BC: .255 CORRECTED: .314				BC: .255 CORRECTED: .314		
VELOCITY: 3200.0 FPS				VELOCITY: 3200.0 FPS		
SIGHT HEIGHT: 2.0				SIGHT HEIGHT: 4.5		
CROSS WIND: 10 MPH				CROSS WIND: 10 MPH		
ZERO RANGE: 50				ZERO RANGE: 50		
+1.1 @ 100 YARDS				+3.6 @ 100 YARDS		

DIST	PATH	DRIFT		DIST	PATH	DRIFT
50	+0.0	0.2		50	+0.0	0.2
100	+1.1	0.9		100	+3.6	0.9
150	+1.1	1.9		150	+6.1	1.9
200	−0.1	3.5		200	+7.5	3.5
250	−2.5	6.0		250	+7.5	6.0

There are numerous barrel twist rates available in factory rifles, and they should be matched with the proper ammo.

In the 5.56mm, twist rates of 1 turn in 12 to 13 inches are well suited for bullets in the 52-to-55-grain category. A barrel twist rate of 1 turn in 9 inches will handle most bullets from 55 to 69 grains. A barrel twist rate of 1 turn in 7 inches is more suitable for the bullets in the heavier weight range, 62 to 69 grains. The idea is to spin the bullet just enough to stabilize it. Heavier bullets need more spin to remain stable in flight. Without proper stabilization, inaccuracy results from the bullet's tumbling.

The recoil impulse and the weight of the 5.56mm ammo are light, and the magazine capacity is enough to let the shooter to concentrate on shooting rather than counting rounds and reloading.

by placing the scope sight at the correct height on the rifle. The properly scoped AR-15 rifle allows for a proper no-strain cheek-to-stock weld and correct use from behind, under, and around cover objects. The lower sight height also permits a shallower angle of bullet departure from the muzzle, while still obtaining the desired maximum point-blank range.

The low-scoped AR-15 fired with the same ammunition at the point-blank target results in the POI being less than 2 inches below the POA. At 50 yards, the bullet's impact is precisely zeroed on the POA. At 100 yards, the angle of the bullet's departure results in an impact of 1.1 inches above the precise POA. At 150 yards the bullet's impact is 1 inch above the precise POA. At 200 yards, the bullet impact again intersects the line of sight and is zeroed. At 250 yards, the bullet is 2.5 inches below the exact POA.

What this means for the tactical officer or action shooter requiring a shot out to 200 yards is that a dead-center reticle hold on target will achieve a hit, provided that the target is 4 inches or larger in diameter and that he is considering trajectory only. Wind drift or atmospheric changes also have to be considered. A target 5 inches or larger out to 250 yards could be hit with a center hold using this zero with a low-scoped AR-15 and specified ammunition combination.

Taking the point-blank zero to the realistic fringes of 5.56mm effectiveness permits the midrange rifle's capabilities to overlap with those of the precision rifle's. This is a "just in case" precaution. Most likely the carbine will not be used for targets more than 100 yards. This same point-blank zero makes the carbine effective at these ranges. Less than 2 inches low at point-blank ranges to about an inch high at 100 yards, you fire POA, POI on all but the smallest of targets. And by knowing your trajectory pattern you can make quick, minor hold compensations for even more precise shooting. For example, it is essential to remember that when shooting at 25 yards you must hold 1 inch over the desired POI to compensate for the bullet's trajectory.

Other calibers, ammunition, and rifle systems require detailed evaluation of their point-blank range capabilities. Low sight heights and flat-shooting trajectories are a good combination for maintaining trajectory on a limited target out to medium ranges.

Shooters considering using Federal's 69 BTHP Match .223 load should test it thoroughly before using it in semiautomatic firearms. It is an accurate load but more suited to the properly twisted .223 bolt gun than the semiautomatic. The bullets are not cannelured and have a flat spot on the nose. Sometimes the light neck tension on the case will not hold the bullet securely enough to withstand the feeding cycle on a semiautomatic weapon. A bullet that pushes back in the case can stop the action or cause high pressures if fired. The Federal Premium .223 load featuring Nosler 55-grain, ballistic-tip, cannelured bullets overcomes these problems. This load is accurate and reliable and has moderate penetration.

SPECIFIC-RANGE ZEROING

This procedure is more suited for use with a precision rifle. A precision rifle should be capable of delivering bullets on target at all practical ranges. This means that you don't allow the trajectory of the bullet to determine how high or low from the POA the bullet will strike. This zeroing procedure enables you to zero in on the exact POA that you want to hit. This takes knowledge, skill, and equipment—but most of all, knowledge.

To limit the example, we will use a bolt-action precision rifle in .308 Winchester caliber, shooting a 168-grain BTHP bullet at 2,500 fps. The BC of the bullet is .475 corrected to .574 for our hypotetical location. The sight height of the rifle we are shooting is 1.5 inches above the bore. The scope is a variable 6.5–20x.

You want your precision rifle to overlap with the capabilities of your midrange carbine because the heavier caliber may be required at close range in situations requiring barrier penetration. Make sure your precision rifle's scope will focus while in close. The standard zero point will be set at 100 yards. Beyond this point, the intersection of bullet and sightline will be dialed in. At ranges closer than 100 yards the bullet and sightline will be very close and compensated for by holding as needed.

If you expect to obtain good data from this zeroing process, calm conditions, a stable rest, duty match-grade ammunition, a rifle set up with a quality repeatable scope, and excellent personal marksmanship skills are all required. Calculations and compensations may have to be made for your immediate environment if the zeroing process is completed outside your region. If you obtained your data while working on a range outside your region, check your 100-yard zero when you return to your home base. Make necessary adjustments to perfect the zero and reset your elevation turret to the zero mark. From this point, dial in different ranges and confirm their accuracy.

All your equipment and ammunition should have been tested and evaluated prior to this point for reliability, repeatability, and accuracy. If it has not, do so before going any further. Information gained will not be reliable if you are not using an accurate, repeatable system. Any time you change equipment or ammunition you will need to do the zeroing process all over. Recommended cleaning procedures should be followed throughout the process.

Align the scope with the bore by using the collimator, or you can bore-sight the rifle. Bore-sighting is a simple process whereby you remove the bolt assembly from the rifle and look down the bore at a distant target. Solidly bag the rifle into position on a bench and confirm that you can still see the target through the bore. Don't bump the rifle while looking through the scope. Adjust the cross hairs onto the target. This will give you a rough zero.

This is the beginning of a long and detailed data-gathering process. Note the variety of targets for comparison sight pictures.

This chart indicates actual values of 1/8 and 1/4 MOA clicks out to 1,000 yards. A shooter using field-expedient click value determinations can be very close to actual values. For example, at 600 yards one click equals 6/4, or 1 1/2 inches per click. The actual value is 1.57 inches.

RANGE YARDS	CLICK VALUE IN INCHES	
	1/8	1/4
25	0.03	0.07
50	0.07	0.13
75	0.10	0.20
100	0.13	0.26
125	0.16	0.33
150	0.20	0.39
175	0.23	0.46
200	0.26	0.52
225	0.29	0.59
250	0.33	0.65
275	0.36	0.72
300	0.39	0.79
325	0.43	0.85
350	0.46	0.92
375	0.49	0.98
400	0.52	1.05
425	0.56	1.11
450	0.59	1.18
475	0.62	1.24
500	0.65	1.31
525	0.69	1.37
550	0.72	1.44
575	0.75	1.51
600	0.79	1.57
625	0.82	1.64
650	0.85	1.70
675	0.88	1.77
700	0.92	1.83
725	0.95	1.90
750	0.98	1.96
775	1.01	2.03
800	1.05	2.09
825	1.08	2.16
850	1.11	2.22
875	1.15	2.29
900	1.18	2.36
925	1.21	2.42
950	1.24	2.49
975	1.28	2.55
1000	1.31	2.62

Another method of achieving a rough one-shot zero is to aim at the center of the target and fire one round. Reaim at the center of the target and hold the rifle in a steady position. Move the cross hairs to the center of the bullet hole and you have a rough zero.

Set up a target at 25 yards and fire a three-shot test group. All firing should be done from your most stable field position (and, of course, this should also be the position you use the most). For most marksmen, this position will probably be prone, off a quality bipod, with rear stock support.

The 25-yard test group should be a "one holer." This shot group should be moved into the center of your aiming point by adjusting your scope. Once this is complete, fire another test group to confirm the zero is centered exactly. This is easier to achieve at 25 yards than at longer ranges because of possible wind interference. It should be emphasized throughout that zeroing must be done in calm conditions to obtain "no wind" zero.

It is best to use an assistant when making your target movements to new, predetermined distances so that you can keep your breathing rate low and concentrate on your shooting. The distances should be specifically *measured*, not paced. The shooting range should be across level ground.

Have the target moved to a point 100 yards downrange and fire another three-shot group. The group should be centered on target. Make any minor elevation changes needed to get the group exactly zeroed for 100 yards. Your 6.5–20x scope has 1/4-MOA adjustments. This means your impact point will move .261 inch per click at 100 yards. The value "per click" changes as the range increases. A rough estimate of how much value a click will have can be made by considering each click to be worth 1/4 inch of movement at 100 yards, rather than a true 1/4 MOA. At 100 yards, the value per click is approximately 1/4, at 200 yards the value per click is approximately 1/2, at 300 yards the value of one click is approximately 3/4, etc. This is a field-expedient method of determining necessary ups and downs. For example, you have estimated the range of a target at 400 yards, dialed in the required amount of elevation, and fired. Your spotter advises that your bullet impact was 5 inches low. You know your hold was solid, so you must determine how many clicks up it will take to put you on target. Your target is 400 yards away, so this means that one click equals 4/4 of inch per click; therefore, each click is worth 1 inch. The total number of clicks required to raise you 5 inches at 400 yards is 5. At 600 yards, each click is worth 6/4, or 1 1/2 inches per click, etc. True MOA calculations would require you to multiply 6 (on a 600-yard target) times .261 inch. This shows the exact value per click to be 1.56 inch. This is handy to determine to calculate how many clicks it takes to get centered, but mathematical field calculation should be avoided whenever a simpler method is possible.

Center your shot group and confirm its exactness by firing another group. If minor adjustments are required, make them, and fire another shot group for confirmation.

At this point, you must determine how far you want your dial-in capabilities to extend. A 100-yard zero and the capability of dialing in out to 500 yards should be no problem with your .308 Winchester and 6.5–20x scope. Reliable hits beyond this range with this rifle-scope-ammo system will depend on how your scope is mounted and how much elevation adjustment it has left after your 100-yard zero. Standard scopes are quite limited in the adjustments, and long-range shooting may require mounting modifications to achieve the desired results.

The turret on most scopes will go on clicking beyond the point where the scope has stopped making internal adjustments, so don't be fooled by audible clicks.

A simple way to determine how many clicks actually make internal adjustments is by installing your collimator and watching the clicks being made through the scope. Count how many clicks you observed to calculate reticle movement. This will give you the total amount of elevation adjustment available from the scope mounted in its current position. Compare this with a computer-generated drop chart prepared for your cartridge and determine how far out this adjustment will take you from your 100-yard zero.

Another method of checking the accuracy and degree of your elevation adjustment is to place a 10-foot-tall piece of butcher paper at 100 yards. At the bottom of this paper place an aiming point. Fire a 100-yard zero confirmation group into this. Once zero is confirmed, fire a single shot at regular intervals in turret adjustment, such as every 16 clicks. When the hits stop rising, you have reached your limit of elevation. The distance can be measured to determine total elevation available beyond the 100-yard zero. At this point, you can also measure the distance between shot impacts to check click consistency. Shoot at the same intervals on the way back down. The same number of clicks should place your last shots back in your beginning shot group, provided that both you and your scope are performing reliably.

A comparison of total elevation adjustment to the maximum distance you want to dial in on will determine whether you will proceed from your 100-yard target to 150 yards or return to your armorer for rifle changes. There is no need to waste valuable time and ammunition if your scope will not allow adjustment to the required distance. Removing and adjusting the scope's mount necessitates that the scope be rezeroed, invalidating any information obtained beforehand.

A rifle-scope-cartridge combination that will not perform reliably out to the desired distance must be changed. The scope may be replaced with a model allowing more elevation adjustment. The scope base may be altered to allow for more use of existing adjustments, or a new cartridge or bullet weight with a flatter trajectory may be needed to make the desired range with existing adjustments.

We will say, for sake of continuing the illustration of the .308 Winchester, that we changed scopes to the 20x Leupold Ultra with generous amounts of elevation. Assume also that we modified the scope's mounting base to allow for

.308 Winchester trajectory compensation all the way to 1,000 yards for information purposes.

Repeat the close-range zeroing procedures and get the 100-yard zero reestablished with the new mount-scope combination. Set your turret to indicate zero at 100 yards. Dial in at ranges more than 100 yards, but leave the scope turret at the 100-yard zero for shots less than 100 yards. Remember, being able to shoot at ranges under 100 yards with the precision rifle is still critical if you want to overlap its capabilities with those of the midrange carbine.

With the 100-yard zero established, set up and fire groups at targets located at 25, 50, and 75 yards. Information from these targets will determine sight-hold compensations at distances closer than 100 yards.

The .308 Winchester cartridge you are shooting, with a sight height of 1.5 inches, typically shoots less than 1 inch off the sightline when zeroed at 100 yards and fired at closer ranges. Required close-range compensation should be minimal.

Before proceeding beyond this point, you need to log some important information that you have developed. Write in your field notebook which rifle and scope you are using, complete with serial number. Log the ammunition you are using, including lot number, time, date, temperature and other weather conditions, and the range facility and altitude at which you zeroed. Install your collimator in your rifle zeroed for 100 yards and read the grid. Sketch an identical grid in your log book and plot the 100-yard zero cross hair location. Label it as such. *Important*: any time you use a collimator in the field with live ammunition, remember to remove the spud from the bore before firing.

Your zero target should be of the correct dimensions to simulate the target at which you expect to shoot. The police marksman should use a full-sized, lifelike human target; the deer hunter, a full-sized, lifelike deer target; the IPSC shooter, a regulation target, etc. For consistent shot groups, this zero target should have a precise aiming point. This could be accomplished with a bull's-eye-type target, of course, but this would not give the shooter needed ranging information. Ranging information by scope reticle comparison should be obtained at all ranges from 25 yards and beyond. Also be sure to log the reticle holds necessary to make precise hits on the 25-, 50-, and 75-yard targets.

Accurate range estimation is critical to accurate shot placement, and even more so with rainbow trajectory calibers. An extreme example is the .308 Winchester at 1,000 yards. Misjudging a 1,000-yard range to be 950 yards will result in an additional 52 inches of bullet drop—and this is only a 50-yard error. Recording accurate range reticle comparison sketches in your field data book or acquiring precision RF equipment will help you make accurate range estimates.

Shooters using a duplex cross hair or a D & L tactical reticle should place one of the thick-post points at a specific location on the full-sized target. Make note of where another reticle point is located, and you have a reticle reference for that size target at that specific range.

It is important to remember that with a standard variable-magnification scope, the magnification must be maintained on a single power setting when taking all of the readings for your reticle comparison sketch. When making range estimations using the reticle-comparison method, the power must be the same as you used when making your sketch. This is the only way that it can be accurate; the target image goes up and down in size with magnification changes. You don't have to worry about this with fixed-power scopes and custom variable-magnification scopes with the reticle in the first focal plane; in the latter, the cross hairs enlarge consistently with the target image.

Log a sketch of the images you received at 25, 50, 75, and 100 yards in your field notebook. Be sure to note that the images were taken with the scope set on 20x or whatever magnification you decide to use.

Now that you have confirmed required close-range trajectory-compensation hold requirements, ascertained what a 25-, 50-, 75-, and 100-yard target looks like on 20x, and sketched these images, you can have your target moved to 150 yards, while keeping your 100-yard zero on the scope.

The target should not be moved in increments larger than 50 yards, and 25-yard increments yield even more accurate data. Shooters with precision range-finding equipment may want to interpolate this data into 5-to-10-yard increments so that they will not lose bullet hits at long ranges in cases where the bullet's drop is substantial. The target should be backed by a large, fresh backer, such as a new 4-by-8-foot piece of plywood.

Fire an accurate shot group at the 150-yard target while maintaining your 100-yard zero. Your assistant, now equipped with a walkie-talkie, informs you how far below center the shot group is located. Take this opportunity to practice determining how many clicks up it will take to put you on target. At 100 yards, a click is worth approximately 1/4 inch; at 200 yards, 1/2 inch, etc. That means that at 150 yards, a click is approximately 3/8 inch.

Collimator zero.

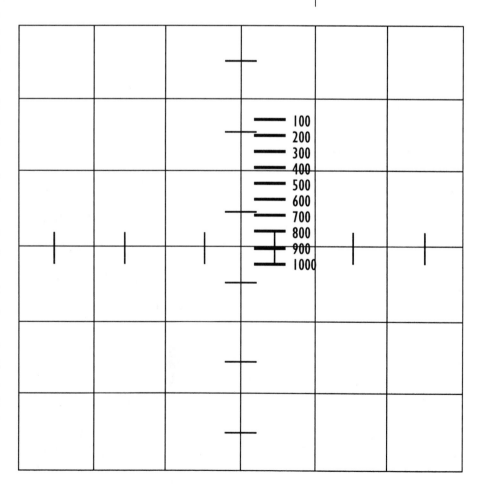

Click up, shoot, and check. A radio-equipped assistant makes it easy. You will probably need to fire a couple of groups at each range to center the group exactly. Once centered, log the exact number of clicks required to achieve the 150-yard zero point from the 100-yard zero point. You don't need to use MOA or any other more complicated method. Simple clicks are best. Don't worry about the value per click; all you need to know is the number of clicks required.

Log the number of clicks it will take to get from the 100-yard zero to your 150-yard zero. Sketch the reticle target image while on 20x into your logbook and mark it as the 150-yard image. Install your collimator and plot the 150 yard zero in your logbook.

Have your assistant move

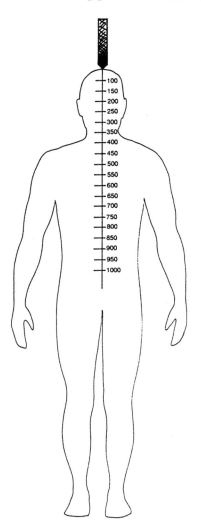

Example of logbook reticle-comparison plotting for range estimation (not to scale).

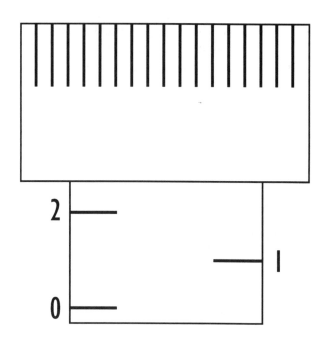

(Above) Example of 100-yard zero turret appearance.

(Below) Reticle-comparison data book plotting is also applicable to objects commonly found at the site of a tactical incident. An example would be a vehicle parked in front of the residence in question. With logbook comparison data on a common-size of vehicle tire, the range can be estimated and dialed in before a suspect appears. Position a tire beside your zeroing target and log the data as you do with your human-form target.

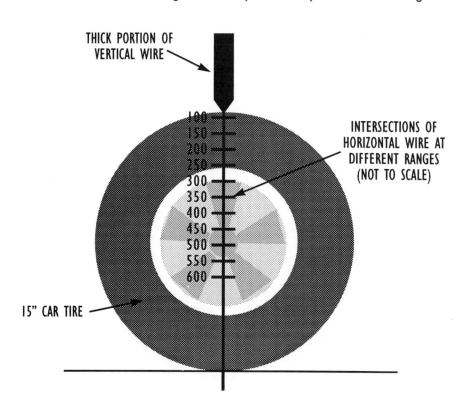

your target and backer to 200 yards and repeat the procedure. Fire a 200-yard shot group with the 150-yard zero and move up the required amount to center the group. Logging the total number of clicks it takes you to get from the 100-yard zero to the 200-yard zero will make your job easier later on. Don't simply log the number of clicks it takes to get from 150 to 200 yards.

Sketch the 20x reticle target image from 200 yards into your logbook. Plot your collimator reading in your logbook. Have your assistant move the target to 250 yards and complete the same procedure.

Remember, the number of clicks it takes to get to a target should be the number of clicks

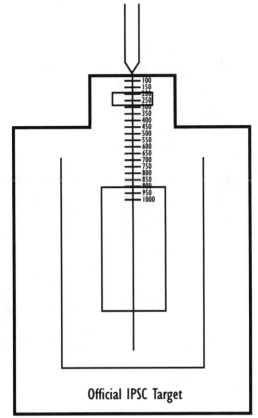

Official IPSC Target

Another field-practical method of range estimation that works well with duplex scopes is to indicate a specific point on an expected target and then note where the horizontal cross hair is positioned on target. This all falls under data development on your known distance range. Different targets and magnification scopes will, of course, affect the diagram developed. Data development and range-estimation readings must be made at the same magnification.

Shooters should not interchange meters and yards. The conversion chart, rounded off to 5-yard increments, indicates how much difference there is between two measurements.

CONVERSION FORMULAS
Yards to meters: yards x .9141 = meters
Meters to yards: meters x 1.094 = yards

Yards	Meters	Yards	Meters
50	45	130	120
55	50	135	125
60	55	140	130
65	60	145	130
70	65	150	140
75	70	200	180
80	85	300	275
85	80	400	365
90	80	500	455
95	85	600	550
100	90	700	640
105	95	800	730
110	100	900	820
115	105	1,000	915
120	110	1,500	1,370
125	115	2,000	1,830

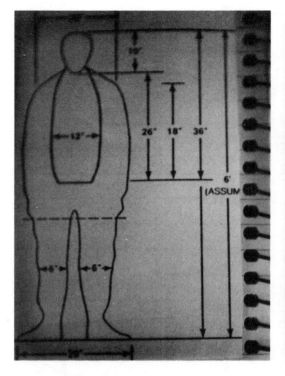

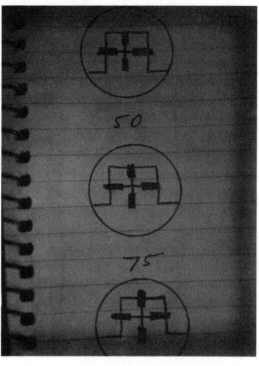

Information from a marksman's data book should contain information pertaining directly to his personal shooting system and the type of target encountered. Waterproof data books are recommended.

it takes to get there from your *100-yard* zero. The reasoning for this is simple and field effective: if you carry your rifle on the 100-yard zero mark and get called out to make a 300-yard shot, simply click in the required clicks to take you from a 100- to a 300-yard zero. You can further simplify "dialing in" by marking the zeros directly on the turret.

Follow this procedure all the way out to the maximum distance for which you will be responsible, farther if possible. The required clicks, collimator readings, and target/reticle images should be logged for each distance. Even though truly long-range shots are rare, the information and experience increase your understanding of bullet flight.

Click back down the required number of clicks to return to your 100-yard zero while watching your collimator grid. The grid reading should be back on the 100-yard plot. Fire another group at 100 yards. If you have counted correctly and your scope is operating properly, your 100-yard group will be centered on the first try.

When you train at distances beyond your zero range and readjust your scope to do so, you should always return to your 100-yard zero and fire a confirmation group.

Zero confirmations should be a regular part of your shooting routine, whether it be with rifle, handgun, shotgun, or submachine gun. These confirmations can be done at closer distances when a long-range facility is not available, provided you know the trajectory of your bullet. Say, for example, that you are put on standby for a call-out, and the only available range is a 25-yard pistol range. To maintain confidence in your weapons and ensure that there has been no change in the zero, you fire at 25 yards with a 100-yard zero. Going back to your logbook, you compare your bullets' 25-yard impact with a confirmed 100-yard zero impact. If your 25-yard impact is the same as previously logged when your 100-yard zero was confirmed, you are still zeroed.

The same can be done with the carbine.

In situations that don't allow for live-fire zero confirmation, your collimator and logbook plot information can be used for visual confirmation.

Wind deflection is a critical element in your shot calculation. This information should also be contained in your logbook. Without scientifically controlled environments, this information is difficult to obtain in the field-zeroing process. The best source of wind drift information, as of this writing, comes from a computer. You

Attach a synopsis of developed data to your rifle for field-expedient use.

feed exact cartridge information into the computer, and you get drift information in the requested increments. If you don't have access to a computer, you can obtain fairly reliable information from a reputable reloading manual. Wind is an ever-changing condition, as is its effect on your bullets' flight. Because it is not a constant, I prefer using a tactical reticle for hold-off compensation, rather than clicking in windage compensation. Simply know the value of your windage dots at all ranges and apply the correct amount of wind drift compensation.

You should devote specific sections in your logbook to wind drift, atmospheric changes, angle shooting, and trajectory. All this information should be confirmed on the range before it is relied upon in the field. Drop, windage, lead, angle, and weather charts are normally quite reliable, but everything should be confirmed by you before mission call-out.

By following these procedures, you should have excellent and reliable information in your logbook. Copies of this information should be made in case you the logbook gets lost or damaged. A brief summary of the logbook data should be contained somewhere on your rifle. This quick-reference material should be laminated, waterproofed, and taped onto the scope or stock, or kept in a sling bag. If you are required to go into a situation cold, simply use your reticle patterns or range finder to estimate the range; dial in the zero; confirm the new zero on your collimator; address the wind, temperature, and angle; and make the shot.

Rifle Marksmanship

JUST READING THIS BOOK WILL NOT MAKE YOU A MARKSMAN. ALL THE LATEST equipment, most accurate ammunition, finest optics, and good intentions in the world will not put rounds consistently on target. You must work at developing your personal marksmanship skills.

You must be proficient at basic marksmanship before attempting advanced skills. This is an area where you must be brutally honest with yourself. Many people have difficulty acknowledging that their personal skills are lacking and instead prefer to blame other things. It seems to be much easier to say that the equipment was faulty, the conditions were bad, or "these bullets just don't shoot straight." This can often lead to time and money being wasted trying to correct nonexistent equipment problems and, if changes are made, less familiarity with the equipment you are using, hence even worse performance.

A shooter who cannot consistently shoot at or close to the mechanical performance level of his accurate equipment will not be able to develop accurate, reliable data. This problem can also occur when a skilled marksman is equipped with less than accurate equipment. Combine poor equipment with poor basic marksmanship skills, and you complicate the matter even more. Reliable data can only be developed from a competent marksman using accurate equipment.

After acquiring top-quality, accuracy-proven equipment, if your targets are still not showing you the mechanical accuracy that the equipment is capable of, you must improve your personal training and skills. Professional instruction greatly reduces your personal training efforts by teaching you how to avoid mistakes. Learning from another's experience lets you bypass the time and expense it would take you to work your way through similar problems. This is true whether developing shooting skills or selecting equipment. This way, you get into the performance learning curve in the quickest possible time.

Review and apply the following information to your basic marksmanship skills. Proper technique applied to a well-positioned, accurate rifle should achieve excellent shot groups. Tight groupings will indicate that the shooting system of the rifle, ammunition, scope, and shooter is performing correctly. Small shot groups are not

103

the ultimate goal for the tactical marksman but are a stepping-stone toward the one-shot, one-hit goal. Benchrest shooters have demonstrated amazing feats of group shooting at known distances on ranges complete with wind flags and spotter targets—luxuries not available to the tactical marksman. You must apply the following marksmanship skills to attain benchrest accuracy performance and then combine the basic skills with advanced techniques to calculate and fire single shots under field conditions.

SIGHT ALIGNMENT

This section analyzes sight alignment as it relates specifically to telescopic sights. Scope sight alignment is simpler than the multiple eye shifts required for open sight alignment.

The scope sight allows the shooter to basically contain both front and rear sights in one point, the reticle. Having a single focal point greatly simplifies the sight alignment on the target for the scope-trained shooter.

Throughout his chapter, I will take for granted that the shooter's rifle is reliable, accurate, and properly zeroed, thus allowing concentration on marksmanship rather than the mechanics of the firearm.

To align the scope sight on target, the shooter must obtain the proper eye relief behind the ocular lens and center his vision through the scope. A view through the scope that is not "full" means that there is not a full field of view visible; rather, there is a shadow ring all the way around the field of view. An improper field of view could indicate that the scope is too close or too far from the shooter's eye. A scope too close to the shooter's eye not only interferes with the field of view but could hit the shooter during recoil. This could cause injury, and a bleeding eyelid obviously affects rapid follow-up shots.

An uncentered eye position behind the ocular lens is indicated by a half-moon shadow around one of the edges of the field of view. This can lead to problems placing bullets on target. Off-center aiming results in bullet impact in the direction opposite the one shadow is on. Correct head position behind the scope is very important to achieving this centered view through the scope.

A bright, focused, centered, full field of view—combined with the scope's magnification—allows for precise reticle (or sight) alignment on the target. For best performance, your eye's focus point should be the aiming point of the reticle that you are using for the particular shot. In most cases it is the center intersection of the reticle. The center of the reticle should be considered the front sight of an open iron sight combination, and be your point of concentration. In the case of a scope reticle with windage hold-off marks on the horizontal cross hair, your focus point may be one of these marks or between these marks.

The scope sight brings the target into the same focal plane as the reticle. This simplifies things and eliminates the need to repeatedly shift focuses between sight and target to ensure alignment. Simply stated, the reticle will appear to be superimposed on the target. All that is required of the shooter to align this sight picture is that he properly place his eye behind the scope and focus on the aiming point of the reticle, while placing it on the desired impact point of the target.

Holding the sight picture at the desired impact point on the target throughout the entire process involves additional concerns. It is humanly impossible to hold the rifle dead still without support. A wavering rifle means a moving sight picture. This, of course, means that the desired impact point is not being maintained. Top off-hand shooters (those who shoot with their firearms unsupported by artificial means) can attain incredible accuracy through dedicated practice, but truly precise shooting can only be attained by using a solid rest.

The difficulty of the shot dictates how much support is required to make the shot. The more precise the shot must be, the more precise the hold has to be. The accomplished shooter can make simple shots from off-hand positions, but provided that time is not a critical factor, added support for even a simple shot means added precision and reliability.

There are several ways to achieve shooting support. Some are quicker to acquire, but are less stable; others take longer to assume, but offer greater support. Being familiar with all the common positions and how to assume them quickly makes you effective in most situations. Being experienced with different positions helps you fit the position to the situation and determine if the shooting position provides enough support to accomplish the required shot. Being experienced in multiple shooting positions will allow the shooter to be effective in many environments and make good use of available cover and concealment.

When using positions of bone support only, make sure the rifle will stay on target without muscular persuasion. Align your body so the rifle naturally points at the target. This produces the fastest follow-up shots after recoil.

Rule of thumb: Always obtain the most stable shooting support practical for the situation. Cover, concealment, and field of fire should be some of your considerations when selecting which position to use.

OFF-HAND SHOOTING

Off-hand shooting should be avoided in live situations. If true precision is required, the off-hand position probably will not provide the necessary support. Off-hand shooting may be the only option in certain situations, so training in its use is recommended.

Shooters whose ammunition budget accommodates serious off-hand shooting training can achieve skill at the position and gain more confidence when they go to supported positions. Shooting supported after training off-hand gives the shooter a rock-solid feel for the supported positions. However, if your match ammunition supply is extremely limited, training in the off-hand position should be limited. Results from the off-hand position yield only questionable data at best. Shooting situations requiring quick shots from an off-hand position will most likely fall into close-to-medium-range encounters. Handling these off-hand shooting situations is much easier and probably more accurate with a midrange carbine. Its light weight, light recoil, and semiauto action make it much more suitable for the task. The awkwardness of the heavy bolt rifle in quick off-hand shooting is a hindrance.

The accurized bolt rifle always has the advantage in mechanical accuracy, but quick off-hand shooting normally favors usable practical accuracy.

The type of rifle you are shooting and the speed with which you must shoot, along with the target you must hit, dictate the best off-hand technique. With the heavy rifle on a precise target, the rifle requires support throughout the entire trigger pull to register a hit. I have found that the best way to achieve this without artificial support is with weak-hand support under the stock. The weak hand should be palm up under the magazine area of the action, and the weak arm elbow should be under the hand, supported by the torso. The strong hand should be on the pistol grip. The strong-arm elbow should be down alongside the torso for support so that there are no flailing limbs to disturb the hold. On quick, close, not-so-precise shots with the heavy rifle, more of a standard forearm-pistol grip hold should be used. Be sure to break the shot when the sight is aligned and before fatigue causes you to waver. Aggressively snap the rifle into position, align the sights, and fire.

SUPPORTED STANDING

Shooting from a standing supported position is substantially better than off-hand shooting without support. A sling or artificial support can add much stability to this position.

You need to keep your sling positions practical. Don't assume that you will be able to wear a tight sling while covering a target area for 12 hours; buckling yourself into a competition sling is not practical in the field. Your sling system must be quick and easy, for both getting into and out of. It should be used to supplement unsupported shooting when nothing more stable is available.

Practicing unsupported shooting with the heavy rifle gives the shooter a feeling of rock solidness when he changes to supported shooting.

A standard hasty sling position is OK, but the D.L. sling is better. Both sling setups can be used quickly in almost any position. Simply adjust the hanging loop, which is created by the sling when it is attached at the two forearm points, to a length that lets you insert your support arm, make one wrap, and grasp the unsupported forearm. Full tension can be used when firing a rifle with a free-floated barrel and reinforced swivel studs. Sling-shooting a rifle such as a non-free-floating AR-15 should be done with care to prevent disturbing the point of impact. Light sling tension and a straight back pull from the front sling hanger under the palm of the support hand are in order.

For shooting while standing, a solid barricade is another means of stabilizing a sight hold. Avoid any contact with the support by the barrel because this disturbs barrel vibrations and affects accuracy. Your weak hand should be in contact with the support. Hold the rifle's forearm like a pool cue while gripping the support to steady the front end of the rifle. Take a wide leg stance and a locked-in elbow position to steady the rear end of the rifle. Don't attempt to lean into any barricade that you have not confirmed to be solid. Be prepared to maintain your balance at all times. Whenever the "pool-cue" hold is not suitable, place your weak-arm forearm against the barricade.

Standing with solid support under the forearm is the next step up in support. Remember not to place support under the barrel, only under the forearm. Use a soft support under the forearm, such as a coat or mat. If this is impossible, use your weak gloved hand as support under the forearm. To minimize jump on recoil, don't rest the forearm against a hard surface.

SQUATTING ("RICE PADDY POSITION")

This position is simple and quick to assume. From a standing position, with your feet approximately one step apart, simply squat low and place the backs of your elbows on the fronts of your knees. Additional support and quickness can be achieved by using a sling. This position gives the shooter a lower profile, while still permitting him to shoot over knee-deep grass. Grasping any available coarse vegetation with the weak hand and holding

The "rice paddy" squat is quick and relatively stable.

Proper light selection and positioning allow instant on-off operation while you keep your hands in shooting position.

tension between the vegetation and the forearm can add even more support when in this position.

KNEELING

Shooting from a kneeling position can range from standard bone support to most of the stability options discussed above.

Kneeling without artificial support should be done with full bone support. Get as much ground contact as possible with your strong-side lower leg. If your body style permits it, the entire length from your knee to your foot should be in contact with the ground. Your weak-side leg should have the knee elevated and the foot planted on the ground. Your weak-side elbow should gain sup-

port from your weak-side elevated leg. You should avoid direct elbow-knee joint contact because this ball-on-ball contact is unstable.

Quick movement in and out of the kneeling position presents no problem for most physically fit shooters.

Sling and solid support can supplement this position as well.

SITTING POSITION

The sitting position is favored by some shooters and cursed by others. Getting in and out of this position quickly is difficult for most shooters. Being inflexible or overweight complicates this matter even more. Supporting your elbows inside your knees is effective for some shooters. Others will experience substantial back strain by bending forward in this manner. Tactical officers who wear wide-coverage ballistic vests may find this position awkward because of interference from the vests.

I have found that the sitting position works best when the back is supported against solid support, the elbows are supported inside the knees, and the rifle is supported by a D.L. or hasty sling.

PRONE POSITION

The prone position has proved very stable and is probably the preferred shooting position among field marksmen seeking precise shot placement. The prone position is possible with only bone support or with artificial supplementation.

If you opt for bone support in this position, you should get both elbows in contact with the ground. One hand should grip the pistol grip while the other supports the forearm. A top-quality shooting jacket or elbow and knee pads make this position substantially more comfortable. The bone-supported prone position can easily be supplemented by a D.L. or hasty sling.

Real precision in the prone position comes when artificial support is added. A mechanical rest, bipod, sandbag, or field-expedient rest gives excellent performance. A bipod is probably the most field practical because it is light, adjustable, and easily carried and deployed. The bipod works best when the legs are set on a softer surface, such as dirt, instead of a hard surface, such as concrete. A hard surface can make the entire rifle bounce on recoil. If you use a Harris bipod and must shoot it off a hard surface, pop the spring-loaded

The prone bipod position is stable and field practical. Note the mat under the muzzle area to reduce ground blast, an important consideration when setting up your position.

legs out just barely. Do not lock the legs into a stop; rather, let them rest on their spring tension so they can absorb some of the bounce. If you use sandbags for support, consider filling them with fine plastic beads instead of sand to lighten your load.

CONTROLLED BREATHING

All the support given by these positions will not place the bullet on target if other shot-delivery requirements are not met. Delivery of a precise shot requires the shooter to control his breathing to maintain a steady hold and shot release. Aerobic fitness is a big benefit in this area. Having the aerobic capacity to get a heavy load into position and quickly regain a low pulse rate makes for a quicker, more controlled shot.

The old styles of breath control where you took a breath, let half out and held can be improved. Taking advantage of the natural respiratory pause works well. At a normal, untaxed breathing rate, a person will draw a breath and exhale over a period of a few seconds. At the end of this period, there is a pause where no breathing takes place. The lull is a good time to break a precision shot. This lull can comfortably last for up to 10 seconds. Beyond this, oxygen deprivation starts to influence your steadiness so you should resume breathing and wait till the next pause to take a shot. During the time you are breathing normally obtain rough sight alignment. You will then have the entire 10-second pause for final alignment and shot delivery. Proper training with intermittent targets teaches the shooter how to regulate his breathing quickly enough to break the shot under demanding time constraints.

TRIGGER PULL

Correct trigger pull is probably the most important part of shot delivery. Improper trigger pull or a "mash" on the trigger will ruin the effort you put into setting up the shot. How you complete your trigger pull will determine how far off the mark your bullet will strike—it is not uncommon for a bad trigger pull to cause the bullet to miss the target entirely.

A new shooter may be baffled by missed shots. He knows that everything looked as it should when he pulled the trigger, but the shot still missed. Shot anticipation, recoil, and improper follow-through, combined with a questionable trigger pull, can all cause problems. Having a shooting partner or instructor load the rifle with an unknown combination of dummy and live cartridges may help the shooter see what is happening. Pulling the trigger on an unexpected dummy cartridge will allow the flinching shooter to see how far he actually pulled the sight out of alignment. Lasers also show the shooter how far the incorrect trigger pull made the dot go off target.

Consistent trigger pull is something shooters continue to perfect over a lifetime of shooting. It takes diligent practice and experience, during dry fire and live fire. A "snap cap" is recommended for all dry-fire practice. It is a plastic cartridge with a spring-loaded firing pin impact point. It is designed to deter firing pin stress and breakage.

I do not agree with using the term "surprise break" to describe the correct trigger pull. It may be suitable as a training illustration, but the police marksman should either intend to fire or not to fire. Your shot is supposed to be deliberate and controlled, not a surprise.

Trigger movement should be controlled with a steady, increasing pressure until the shot breaks, without disturbing the sight alignment. In a quick shot at a not so precise target, such as in a quick off-hand shot, the sight should be aligned and the trigger snapped while the picture is as perfect as humanly possible. In a situation where there is target or shooter movement requiring the trigger pull to be stopped, the shooter should have enough trigger control to do so. The situation may continue to develop and the trigger pull may be restarted, or it may not require a shot at all. The tactical marksman who has begun a trigger pull and is required to stop without shooting should direct the muzzle in a safe direction before any other trigger manipulation is attempted. Then, he should get off the trigger and raise the bolt into its safe position.

Correct trigger control takes practice, but it is worth the time to do so. Without this skill, accuracy will suffer. With this skill, triggers of various weights and pulls can be effectively managed. A smooth, light, crisp trigger may be easier to manage, but almost all weights can be handled effectively with proper technique. Close-combat weapons do not have sniper-grade triggers, yet their performance is greatly enhanced if the shooter is capable of proper trigger control.

FOLLOW-THROUGH

The shooter's job is not over when the trigger is perfectly released. After the trigger is pulled, the sear releases the hammer or striker, which in turn detonates the primer, thus igniting the powder. The powder burns, generating gases that propel the bullet down the barrel. All of this takes time—not much time, but enough to be important. The shooter who breaks the shot and immediately drops the rifle from alignment will affect the shot placement on target.

Follow-through is the key to minimizing any after-trigger break shot disturbance. Break the shot by squeezing the trigger straight to the rear, and follow through by holding the rifle's sight picture on target as the shot goes off and out. Then immediately operate the action of any nonsemiauto you may be shooting for any required follow-up shots. Follow-up bolt operation should be a routine part of your training to make it a habit for multiple targets or follow-up shots in live situations. In training you should shoot, work the bolt, and then observe. If in training you simply shoot and observe, a live situation may catch you observing a situation calling for another shot, but not having a round chambered.

Professional-grade marksman's rifle with D.D. Ross lugged mount and rigid trigger guard assembly.

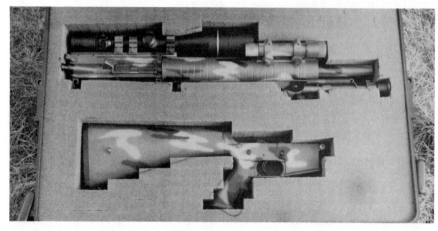

A takedown version of the D & L professional perimeter carbine.

MR-30PG system.

Precision rimfire rifles work well for light elimination and tire deflation.

Close-Action Rifle

DIFFERENT FIREARMS ARE BEST SUITED TO DIFFERENT TASKS. THE DISCUSSION IN THIS chapter centers on what are commonly considered combat weapons. Handguns are for close range; rifles are for long range. There are a few firearms that fall into the middle ground between the two, such as the shotgun, submachine gun, and carbine (midrange rifle).

The shotgun attempts to fill the middle ground with its capability of shooting a variety of projectiles, the most common being shot and slugs. Shot is used for quick and close targets, whereas slugs are best for individual projectile placement and extending the effective range of the shotgun.

Up close, the shot pattern of the shotgun makes hitting the target quick and reliable. The close-range effect of a shot blast certainly contains an abundant amount of energy, but it lacks true precision. A knowledgeable shotgunner can predict his shot pattern fairly reliably and judge the required hold-off to hit a target without hitting a no-shoot target close by. This works fine in training scenarios, but in live encounters something better should be used. A stray pellet, or even a hard-hitting wad, that strikes the face of an innocent or hostage can cause serious injury. The chances of having the luxury of being able to switch to a slug in a shotgun loaded with shot while facing a live situation is slim. Even with the slug, only moderately precise shooting is attainable: 2-to-3-inch groups at 100 yards with iron sights is about as good as it currently gets under field conditions. Considering the problems that quickly present themselves to the tactical officer—and the drawbacks to the limited-ammo-capacity, slower to reload, less than precise shotgun—a better solution should be sought.

A top-quality submachine gun, such as the HK MP5, now available in multiple calibers, can provide a better solution. It allows multiple quick hits, similar to a load

The Benneli Super 90 12-gauge semiauto shotgun is excellent, but I believe that the carbine is more useful to the tactical marksman.

of buck, as well as precise individual shot placement at close range. This is accomplished with a flick of the selector switch, instead of unloading one cartridge and replacing it with another. Its higher ammo capacity allows the shooter to keep his concentration on the situation at hand instead of concerning himself with frequent reloads. The handling and accuracy capabilities of the submachine gun in trained hands make it an excellent close-range weapon. It can reliably hit body targets out to 200 yards, but truly precise iron-sighted bullet placement fades fast after 25 yards. When used for specific applications, such as an entry weapon, its accuracy, low recoil, and moderate penetration work well.

Any shooter wanting to extend the effective operating range beyond that of the submachine gun might want to look at a midrange carbine. A carbine is capable of delivering reli-

A "pool cue" technique with the support hand allows the shooter to grip hard support and pivot the rifle for multiple-target shooting. The rifle should not touch the support because rifle bounce will occur on recoil.

able, fast-handling precision at ranges between that of the pistol and large rifle. Close-to-midrange action is defined as 0 to 250 yards. The accurized carbine is capable of delivering precision shots from point-blank to 200-yards and easy torso hits. This precision, without having to give up the fast-handling, multihit capability at close

Training for shooting from behind cover should strive for as little shooter exposure as possible. Note the use of the pool cue technique of the support hand on the barricade.

When used safely, steel targets are great training aids. The steel must be suited to the cartridge used. An armor-piercing round on this plate damaged the steel.

ranges, makes it an excellent choice for the tactical marksman, as well as the competition shooter and police patrol officer.

Having fewer weapons and trajectories to deal with makes the marksman's job much simpler. Live, close-action shooting demands reliable mechanical accuracy and total familiarity with the trajectory pattern delivered by a specific weapon. Using a very limited number of the best selected weapons and a proper training routine is the best way to accomplish this.

Contrary to some opinions, I prefer the scope sight for close-to-midrange-action carbines. The development of new, optically sighted military combat weapons indicates a trend in this direction as well. The advantages of the scope sight for same focal plane sighting, target ID, shot placement, and low-light shooting have been field proven. This chapter focuses on the effective use of the scoped close-to-midrange-action carbine. Quick, reliable placement of rounds on target is the goal.

(Above) Drop-shooting can give the marksman the shooting angle required to reduce risk to innocent subjects in a close-range situation.

(Above right) Cornering with a shoulder weapon is best accomplished by using a pieing technique.

(Right) The 5.56mm carbine is compact enough for close quarters but still capable of excellent accuracy at medium ranges.

This information should be of interest to the tactical marksman and practical competition shooter alike.

A semiauto or select-fire carbine is suitable for close-to-midrange action, as long as it is used with performance in mind (i.e., for hits on target, not just firing for the sake of firing).

Full-auto in mid-sized rifle cartridges can be very effective, as long as it is restricted to its reliable-hit-probability ranges. A full-auto hand-held carbine can certainly hit a 100-yard target with burst fire, but must-hit center mass shots should be restricted to 25 meters or less. Simply having the capability of full-auto fire can lead the unprofessional shooter into a "spray and pray" mentality. This leads to poor performance and accelerated barrel wear. "Burning out" your barrel is of no benefit when it comes to precision semiauto fire.

Select-fire weapons are effective in the hands of a conservative, well-trained professional, but they are certainly not essential for close-action performance. Civilian ownership and transport of Class III weapons require cutting through a substantial amount of red tape and may make semiautos the best overall selection. There is something to be said for their selector simplicity: safety or fire, no other decisions to be made.

A mid-sized cartridge, like the 5.56mm, provides a low-recoil impulse and fast, aimed follow-up shots. Even though the recoil is low, an aggressive shooting style can be used to allow you to shoot multiple targets faster, maintain your balance, and move from position to position more quickly. If the shooting is very close on multiple targets requiring substantial swing to engage, avoid using any artificial support. This will allow more freedom of

Dedicated precision-rifle practice can slow your close-action skills. To keep your close-action skills sharp, you must practice with your close-action firearms.

movement. The sling should also be secured or removed in order prevent it from catching on things during close action. An alternative to securing the sling would be slinging the carbine submachine gun style. Close-quarter battle (CQB) techniques with the carbine can be performed with the sling in a tensioned submachine gun position. This is especially useful when wearing a gas mask.

Increased ranges require more of a stable platform to make reliable hits. The increased range also reduces the required swing from target to target when they are at the same distance apart as they were at closer ranges. A "pool cue" pivot from solid support is effective for these situations. Grip the solid support with your weak hand while supporting the rifle's forearm with the web of the hand between the thumb and index finger. Use your hand as the pivot point to achieve the necessary supported swing to engage the targets and achieve precise hits.

With the exception of point-blank targets being handled with close-quarter battle (CQB) point-shooting techniques, whenever possible all shooting should be done using conventional sighting and with the stock shouldered. Hip shooting is of limit-

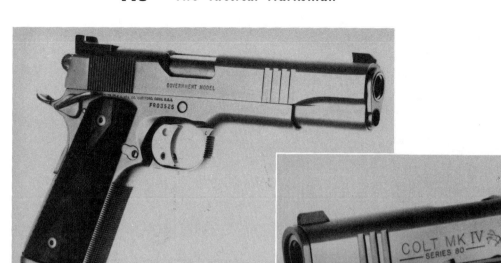

Top-quality backup pistols are a wise investment for tactical operators.

ed value when precise hits are required. A higher underarm assault position is more effective than hip shooting, but proven CQB techniques work better than either. CQB point shooting is most effective when the weapon is brought as close to eyesight line as possible and the rifle is aimed by indexing the turret (or front sight post on iron-sighted weapons) on the target. Targets beyond these point-blank firing ranges are handled with standard reticle alignment.

Your scope sight should be set on its lowest magnification when working on fast, close targets for the widest field of view possible and easy target pickup. To obtain a quick full field of view aligned on target, you should use muscle memory developed through serious training to snap your body, rifle, and scope into alignment with the target.

When assuming your low ready position, do not drop the muzzle past 45 degrees, unless in very close quarters. From this position, the elevation turret on the top of the scope can be used as a rough index point as the rifle is brought into shooting position. Align the elevation turret with the tar-

Special ops pistols may find use by the tactical marksman doing covert close-range intelligence gathering.

Realistic training scenarios go a long way toward successful live-fire performance. The street facade and training tower are part of the Thunder Ranch training facility.

Keeping the muzzle between your eyes and the target area at all times during target search allows you to snap the rifle into position and locate the target in the scope's field of view.

From the low ready position, the target should be located and indicated by the scope's elevation turret. Bring the rifle into shooting position and you will locate the target in the field of view of even higher-powered scopes.

get as the sight comes up. When the sight comes up to its proper eye relief position, you should have a full field of view on target. This technique works well on both low- and high-magnification settings.

From the high ready position, a muzzle-indexing technique works well. The muzzle of the rifle should be interposed between the shooter's eyes and the target. Whenever the eyes move in search of a target, the muzzle should move with the eyes. Care must be taken not to obscure your field of vision during a search using the high ready position. Watch also for low targets.

Locate the target, index with the muzzle, and shoulder the weapon while pushing the muzzle straight out at the target. Watch for the elevation turret to align with the target. This should ensure scope alignment on target once the rifle is shouldered.

SPEED RELOADING

The technique for speed loading varies from rifle to rifle, depending on controls and configuration. Some rifles are quicker than others, especially due to the magazine-seating process. Magazine insertions requiring a two-point latch, such as most of the HKs and the Mini-14, take longer and are more prone to shooter error. During a speed load it is imperative to take the time to double-latch the magazine. The magazine must be seated correctly, or malfunctions will occur.

SPEED RELOADING
1. (Top left) Fire the weapon until it is empty; the bolt automatically locks open when empty.
2. (Top right) Drop spent magazine while acquiring a loaded magazine.
3. (Bottom left) Insert and lock into place.
4. (Bottom right) Slap bolt-release button.

In CQB situations, switching to a secondary weapon for handling an immediate threat can be more efficient than reloading. Once the threat is neutralized, both weapons should be brought back up to full capacity while you are in a position of cover.

The example in the photographs illustrating speed reloading is of the AR-15-style rifle with a detachable-box magazine.

It is time to speed load when you have made the mistake of shooting your rifle dry or the ammo supply in the rifle's magazine is so low that you are going to discard it. When the magazine is dry and the bolt is locked to the rear, getting the rifle back into a ready condition ASAP is your main concern. Whether you drop the empty magazine before or after you have the fresh magazine in hand really makes no difference, unless you are being watched until you run dry. Other than that, don't confuse the magazine retention of the tactical load with the speed load. The procedure for speed-loading the AR-15 is similar to that for the M1911 auto pistol. The bolt automatically locks to the rear on an empty magazine, and the magazine should fall freely by gravity alone when the magazine button is pressed. The magazine-release button is on the right side of the lower receiver, and it is easily activated by the right-hand trigger finger. Hit the button, let the magazine fall, and get a loaded magazine back in the magazine well right away. The left hand should ensure that the magazine is securely locked in place before activating the bolt release. The bolt release is located on the left side of the lower receiver. Don't waste time trying to neatly press it with your finger; slap the side of the rifle with an open palm. The open palm will cover enough area to hit the button without using a single finger to search for it.

The bolt will spring forward at this point and chamber a round. The rifle is then ready to fire. Continue firing or engage the safety. If the encounter is over, retrieve and secure your empty magazine for future use. It should be secured in an area other than with your loaded magazine to avoid a mix-up during another loading. Double-check the chamber to ensure that a round has been chambered, and double-check the magazine to ensure that it is locked in place.

The speed loading procedure should be completed with the trigger finger outside the trigger guard. The reload can be accomplished while the rifle is shouldered, covering a target, or otherwise.

A left-handed shooter can accomplish the same task by activating the magazine release with his right-hand thumb, placing the magazine in the weapon with his right hand, and releasing the bolt with his left-hand trigger finger. You should always remember to maintain your strong hand in a firing grip at all times if at all possible.

THE TACTICAL RELOAD

The tactical reload is completed when the shooter knows his rifle ammo supply is less than full capacity and there is a break in action. The shooter wants to replenish his rifle's ammo supply before continuing any further activity.

You should retain the partially loaded magazine for possible future use. Be careful not to drop it on the ground, to avoid noise or dirt contamination.

The tactical reload should be completed behind hard cover, while maintaining observation on the target area.

Bring the fresh magazine to the rifle before releasing the partially spent magazine. This will create the briefest amount of time for a magazine to be out of the carbine. Should you be required to fire the chambered round while the magazine is out of the weapon, you will have to remember to manually chamber a round out of the fresh magazine after insertion. (The bolt will be forward on an empty chamber because there was no magazine in place to activate the bolt hold-open device.) Drop the partial magazine from the weapon into the palm of your weak hand. This hand should also be holding the fresh magazine. Move the fresh magazine into the magazine well and lock it into place. The bolt will not have to be released or operated if you did not fire the chambered round while the magazine was out. Double-check the chamber to ensure that you have a live round in place. Close the bolt and make sure it goes all the way into battery. This can be quietly accomplished by using the forward bolt assist.

Important note: A magazine loaded to full capacity will be difficult or impossible to lock in place when the bolt is forward. Magazines must be short-loaded by two rounds to allow the magazine to smoothly lock in place.

Place the partially loaded magazine somewhere else than in the pouch where the fully loaded magazines normally go to avoid confusion in the future if a speed reload is required.

Close-action training should also include weapon retention training for both rifle and handgun, as well as equipment-positioning evaluation for close combat. Poor placement and security of support gear, such as distraction devices and knives, can cause them to be used against you.

Malfunction clearance is a very important skill, especially at close ranges where time is critical. Train thoroughly to switch to a secondary weapon for immediate threats. Top-quality weapons and ammunition make malfunctions unlikely, but close action requires preparation for worst-case scenarios.

Failure to fire may indicate an empty chamber or a faulty cartridge. Failure to fire on the second shot normally means that the magazine was not locked in place high enough for the second round to be stripped from the magazine and fed into the chamber.

Both conditions can be corrected by tapping the magazine home, and racking the bolt to chamber a new cartridge. The rifle should then be capable of firing.

Carbine stovepipes, commonly resulting from low-powered ammunition, can easily be corrected by retracting the bolt enough to loosen the empty case, while briskly flicking the rifle to the side, thus ejecting the case. The bolt will then need to be released to finish chambering the next round or retracted to pick up the next round from the magazine, and then released to complete chambering.

Feedway stoppages are best corrected by locking the bolt to the rear, pulling out the magazine, and shaking out any obstructions. The bolt may or may not have to be closed over rounds stuck in the chamber. If the magazine is suspected to be at fault, replace it with a new one on the reload.

Dropping a jammed weapon on the sling and going to the handgun may be the quickest solution to close engagements where you are unsure how to clear the weapon or you have had a mechanical breakdown. The muzzle of the slung weapon must be controlled in case of a hangfire. This condition could make the chambered cartridge fire a few seconds after it has been hit by the firing pin. A properly drop-slung weapon will keep the muzzle pointing in a safe direction, such as at soft ground. Avoid drop-slinging at an upward angle, especially when working closely with a team. A hangfire or cook-off in this position could be disastrous.

Acquiring positions during close action requires aggression and concentration on the primary objective: getting the bullet on target quickly. This is the priority, not

STOVEPIPE CLEARANCE PROCEDURE

Clearing malfunctions from a carbine is not much different than clearing them from a handgun. Failure to fire is commonly caused by failure to fully seat the magazine. Simply tap the magazine into place and rack the bolt to chamber a fresh round.

Feedway stoppages are best cleared by locking the bolt to the rear and removing the magazine. Clear stoppage out of the magazine well or clear the chamber (failure to extract) by racking the bolt over the chamber case and manually pulling it out.

Side stovepiping of an empty case often means low-powered ammunition. Simply retract the bolt while briskly flicking the weapon to the side. The case should fall out, and a new round should be chambered when the bolt is released.

Substantial stoppages with the primary weapon should result in the officer safely dropping the weapon on the sling and going to the handgun. Make sure the muzzle is controlled because a hang-fire can cause the weapon to fire later.

There are causes and cures for every stoppage. If your weapon is malfunctioning, have it fixed before using it for duty.

sliding into position and picking up lost equipment, adjusting your glasses, or licking your wounds. Align the sight and fire; there is no need to wait until the dust settles or even until you stop moving. Some shoot-and-go situations won't even require you to stop.

Close action is physical, and if you let little bumps and bruises bother you, your objective is going to be delayed. Close action requires that you keep your concentration despite any interference. For the competition shooter, this will probably be limited to minor injuries, but for the tactical officer, it may mean performing with substantial injuries, including gunshot wounds.

A fast-action rifle can be demanding on both the shooter and equipment. The carbine is best for protection, while transporting the precision rifle in a protected manner. Note the folding stock on this shooter's weapon. It is certainly more compact for storage, but it is useless in the folded position for a shooter who requires shouldered, aimed fire. The stock should be carried in a usable position for fast-action encounters.

You should learn what happens in close-action shooting during training, practice, and competition. Live experience is a good instructor, but not one that allows many mistakes. Learn and adjust through training. If you find that some of your equipment is not right or won't perform properly

(Left) Training leads to success. Equipment cannot perform to its potential without the assistance of a knowledgeable operator.

under hard use, change it. Don't wait until it fails you in a live situation. If you are distracted by the little things—cacti, scrapes, bruises—equip yourself with protective pads for competition and call-outs.

Your ultimate goal may be to win the match or survive the live encounter.

Acquiring hits on the move is within the reach of the dedicated shooter. Aimed fire from the shoulder gives the best results from all but the closest of distances.

Increasing the odds of doing either requires drive and a never-say-die attitude. If it looks as if you are going down in a live situation, don't go easy and don't go alone!

It is during close-action shooting, movement, and positioning training that your learned techniques become your individual shooting style. Provided that you have done your homework and have attained an acceptable level of muscle memory and physical shooting skill, your body will be able to take over from your mind during fast shooting: your mind will be clear to deal with the decisions required by the situation, and your body will be able to acquire positions and make shots without undue deliberation. These skills are possible by hard-core, continual practice, followed by "pressure-treating" your skills. Realistic training, competition, and live situations will ingrain the skills that you can count on under stress.

Seek out realistic training at every opportunity. IPSC-style rifle competition may have evolved into less realistic scenarios in recent years, but the bottom line is that it still requires making a bullet intersect with a target. Provided you logically separate sport tactics from live-encounter management, you should gain valuable skills in the competition arena. A professional shooter is far from the trigger-happy gun nut some people would have us think. A well-trained shooter, competent and confident in his skills, is less likely to fire in a tense, developing situation than a person who knows that his skills are marginal and feels the need to act sooner than necessary. A well-trained shooter is safer to all involved in a tactical situation.

Practical Rifle Training

TRAINING WILL HAVE TO BECOME A LIFE-STYLE FOR THE TACTICAL MARKSMAN SUBJECT to being called out 24 hours a day, seven days a week. Regular training is necessary to maintain adequate performance. Becoming overconfident and skipping "routine" training will eventually lead to failure.

What many people consider training is simply preparatory range work. Your long-gun system must be chosen, proven, and completely logged before you can expect to use it on call-outs or in realistic training. This means that the rifle, scope, and ammunition combination must perform up to required standards consistently. Your logbook data must be complete with exact information gathered from your specific rifle-scope-ammo combination at known measured ranges. Your range-finding capabilities must be known and proven through known distances, and you must have developed a proven system of wind estimation and compensation. Your 24-hour-shooting capability must be developed and tested through the use of night vision or illumination techniques. This information must be logged for field reference.

Without this information, down to at least 50-yard increments, 10-mph wind divisions, target leads, angle shots, and day/night shooting capabilities, you will simply be guessing at what you are doing.

Obtaining this information takes a lot of time and effort, tempting many shooters to look for shortcuts. If you expect to perform at a professional level, don't minimize your information-gathering efforts.

Shooters without access to a real range facility may think that they have a valid excuse for not fully developing a logbook. If you have a limited range facility, you should make your officer in charge aware, in writing, that you only have reliable information out to a certain number of yards. Make him understand your concerns. Don't guess, even based on drop charts, sniping manuals, or your favorite fortune cookie. Ballistic information that has not been proven in live fire is not suitable for duty use. For example, if your range has a 100-yard capability and you are requested to make a 200-yard shot, you will be attempting something your system has not proven capable of achieving. Guesses that cost innocent people their lives will cost you as well. If you are required to cover longer distances, make time to get to a training center for data development.

Actual training should only begin with a developed system of rifle, scope, ammo, and data. A substantial part of your training from this point forward should be routine data confirmation, which will increase your confidence in your system immeasurably. During data development, you should evaluate your system's ruggedness, reliability, and consistency; but don't stop after one evaluation. You should continue to test your system and confirm the data continually.

Cold shots should be an important part of your training and system confirmation. Carrying your equipment with you in your vehicle on a full-time basis subjects it to many bumps and jolts. Pulling out the rifle time after time and making a cold shot go where it is supposed to will give you the confidence you need to deal with live situations.

Your training here is in cold-shot marksmanship. No warmups, no sighters, just a single shot. Before attempting this shot, you'll get experience in applying your logbook information to calculate the shot. When was the last time you zeroed? What were the conditions? What were the effects on bullet placement? What were the wind, temperature, and weather conditions? The objective is to place the shot exactly, not just close.

Even with a completely reliable system, your POI will vary as a result of shooting conditions. So, just because you were precisely zeroed at 100 yards the last time you left the range does not mean that this is where your bullet will hit the next time. Be especially mindful of wind and temperature conditions, and log effects made by both.

Cold-shot practice at unknown ranges is probably the best training available. This will probably be the most difficult and most frequent shot you are required to make.

APPROXIMATE LEADS FOR 90° MOVING TARGETS
WHEN USING .308 WIN. AMMUNITION*

Yards	Walking Target (2 mph) (lead expressed in feet)	Running Target
100	FRONT edge of target	0.5
200	0.5	1.0
300	1.0	2.0
400	1.5	3.0
500	2.0	4.0
600	2.5	5.0
700	3.0	6.0
800	3.5	7.0
900	4.0	8.0
1,000	4.5	9.0

* NOTE: This chart will differ when using different ammunition. Half-value leads should be used on targets moving at 45°. No lead is necessary for targets moving directly toward or away from the shooter.

Being able to calculate the entire situation and make the hit with one cold shot takes preparation, and this type of training is best done with an assistant. Have the assistant set up the situation in a realistic fashion and give you only basic information. You should be informed of the target's and innocents' descriptions, their approximate locations, and a hasty response plan. Coded radio communication should be established to indicate the need to shoot or not. Standard shooting policies should be in effect for exi-

Realistic field training requires the marksman to calculate the shot with information compiled in his data book. The goal is first-shot hits.

gencies. Your job should be to acquire a good position, calculate the shot, report on any developments in the situation, and make the shot when required.

The shots fired for training purposes should be thoroughly evaluated. This is not blasting time; only precision shooting is allowed. Determine the reasons for any shots missing the mark and make corrections. Common causes for missed shots could include incorrect range or wind estimation, miscalculated atmospheric conditions, and errors in marksmanship. Provided that the logbook information is correct and the shooting system sound, the mistakes are avoidable with sufficient training. If the information is determined to be incorrect, you'll have to recalculate it on a known-distance range.

Misses caused by improper equipment selection should be documented and the equipment changed. In situations where administrators refuse to field correct equipment and attempt to get officers to use inferior equipment, the officers should thoroughly document the matter. Do not let anyone pressure you into using unacceptable equip-

Consistent extended-range performance is obtainable.

ment or attempting actions beyond your documented abilities. It is not uncommon for dedicated marksmen to request training relevant to their task and be turned down because of cost restraints or because the administrators have spent the budget on "fluff" items for themselves. Administrators must understand that shooting is not a natural ability, and that shooting ability does not come from owning or being issued a rifle. Performance comes from serious training, not through limiting the ammunition and training and then ordering a marksman to shoot beyond his capabilities.

Training to shoot in unknown conditions can be accomplished by yourself as well. Simply place a target and move away from it an undetermined distance. You'll have to determine distance, angle, wind, and atmospheric conditions before attempting a shot. The goal should be to calculate the shot from logbook data, confirm any scope compensations on the collimator, and make the shot with one round. Learning this skill out to longer distances, even longer than you'll ever realistically be asked to shoot, gives you more confidence at closer ranges. Training limited to only the statistically average distance will seriously handicap you, even at moderately long distances.

Make a practice of hard training with a high difficulty factor, such as unsupported off-hand shooting. Mastery of this difficult skill will make your rifle seem as if it is cemented to the ground when shooting supported prone.

Occasionally reverse the difficulty to shooting from well-supported positions but with difficult shots, such as small targets behind cover or hostage targets. Learn how to aim at the target, not away from the cover or hostage. This will be a problem with most newer, less confident shooters. But solid training will teach them to trust their equipment and rely on the proven data they have developed.

Frequency of training is also important. Shooters who go to the range once a month and shoot a large quantity of ammo do not gain as much information as those who go more frequently but shoot fewer rounds. Less shooting under more widely varying conditions gives you a better shooting reference and keeps your hand familiar with the trigger.

Formal qualifications should take place once a month, in addition to normal training. The qualification need not entail a lot of rounds; 10 are acceptable. Frequent qualifications in all weather conditions require you to stay sharp at all times, not just to tune up before a semiannual qualification. Your frequent cold-shot practice should be reflected in a superior performance.

Cold-shot and zero confirmation from a solid rest at every training and qualification session should be mandatory. This is true for the carbine and precision rifle, as well as support weapons. Never put away a duty rifle without *knowing* that it is zeroed. Call-outs seem to come at the least expected times.

If possible, it is wise to have an identical backup rifle to your duty rifle. This way, when your main rifle is down for such repairs as rebarreling, you still have a weapon available. This is doubly expensive, but it is ideal for all your equipment. Anytime a secondary firearm is used, even if it is identical to your primary firearm, you must go through a data confirmation process before it is put on duty status.

During tactical training, marksmen should use the actual communications (on secure channels only) they will use in live situations. Any flaws that appear must be eliminated to avoid confusion on call-outs.

Coordinated rifle fire from multiple shooters on a single-shoot signal is realistic training for single or multiple targets. The signal to direct fire should be standardized between the command structure and the marksman and should be kept confidential. Standard green-light orders will alert anyone with a monitor, which could include the suspect as well as the news media.

The sniper commander who directs sniper fire via the radio

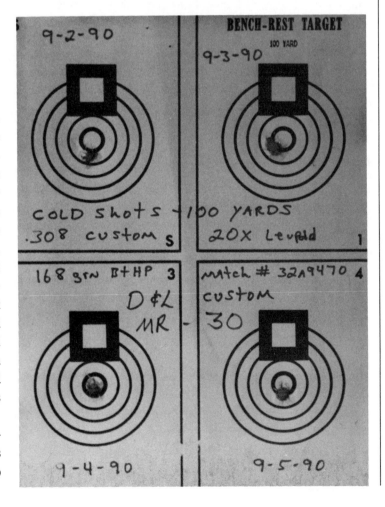

Formal qualifications, job-specific to your particular situation, should be scheduled regularly and should be well documented. Night and long-range qualifications are specifically recommended. The author's 10-shot, 200-yard qualification target.

Consistent accuracy is the goal of the precision rifleman. Cold shots shouldn't vary any more than that of the bullets' flight conditions. With experience, a marksman can calculate and compensate for flight conditions before the cold shot.

must understand the deliberate precision required from the marksman to deliver the shot. Screaming to the sniper over the radio, "Fire, fire, fire!" is not appropriate. For a single marksman to complete a single-shot situation, the commander should give the marksman a coded message to fire as soon as the opportunity presents itself. The marksman can confirm the order and make the shot without further interruption or disturbance.

A simultaneous-shot director will want to confirm that all relevant posts are monitoring and have a target before beginning a simple countdown sequence. In directing simultaneous sniper shots, the shot director's voice should be calm and methodical. Grace under fire is called for during precision shooting. The director should be slow, calm, and methodical, using something like, "5, 4, 3, 2, 1, fire," in order to avoid transferring any shot-disturbing excitement to the shooters. Shooters should train with the commander most likely to be the sniper-fire director. Firing should be done when the word *fire* is actually heard, not anticipated. The shot director may have to call off the shot by putting a stop or halt command in the directions.

You should elevate heart-rate and stress levels before taking the training shot. This will indicate how well you can control your breathing. Do not do run-and-gun courses while actually carrying the precision rifle. Not that it is not rugged, but too much effort has been put into developing the system and related data to risk unnecessary damage. Run to the rifle or run in place, but avoid running with an unprotected precision rifle. The quick-handling carbine can easily be used and protected during running scenarios. Using the carry system developed for the precision rifle and carbine, as you would in a live situation, makes good training sense. The carry bag protects the heavy rifle while en route to the semipermanent post, and the carbine will be available for any emergency close-action shots. If you are required to leave your post to assist other officers, or handle another situation more suited to fast movement and the carbine, the bolt gun should be concealed and disabled before leaving the post. The easiest way to disable the rifle is simply to remove the bolt and take it with you. If at anytime, for any reason, the precision rifle is out of your secured control, confirm the zero before attempting to make any kind of shot or going back into service. This is true in the field, in the armory, or during training.

Some people may not understand how critical the zero is on this weapon and disturb it. Some may do it as a joke in training but fail to realize that it may be needed for a critical shot at any time. Your weapon is *your* weapon; no one else, except an armorer or instructor, should touch it. Even then, rezero before considering it back on duty.

You need night training as well. If you have a third issue rifle set up with a NVD, it requires its own logbook and training regimen. The NVD-equipped rifle has some specific considerations—especially preventing damage to the $5,000 scope. Avoid any dirt and water contamination. Batteries should not be stored in the NVD because battery leakage could damage the scope. Bright light can cause serious damage to an NVD that does not have an automatic shutdown feature. Any daytime zeroing using the daylight cover, or using the scope around bright lights, should be done carefully. Use the same style of zeroing procedure with the night rifle as with the day rifle. Once you have developed the data, routinely confirm and train within unknown-distance scenarios. During use of the night scope, note any muzzle flash plume which can affect your shooting eye's night vision. Your armorer can eliminate the plume through the proper use of flash hider, gunpowder, and barrel length. You must train with any on-duty rifle on a regular basis, including the night rifle. Understand this before you request a third rifle. Too much equipment can make you the proverbial jack-of-all trades but master of none. ITT has just introduced a

Model F 7201 weapon sight. The eyepiece is interchangeable between any day and night optics without affecting zero. Progress is being made with the day-night problem.

Any shooter using the two-gun concept should be proficient at night and low-light shooting. An artificial light source is required under conditions of darkness. With the right training and lighting, daytime accuracy can be obtained easily. Portable, self-contained, battery-powered spotlights can be effective for night shooting. Light from a 500,000-candlepower spotlight can supply enough light on target for shooting in excess of 250 yards. Small, high-intensity, weapon-mounted or hand-held lights can serve beyond 100 yards. Base light selection on performance and rugged simplicity. There are many hand-held spotlights currently available with an excess of one million candlepower; these units have proven to be bright and reliable, but as of this writing they are not self-contained. Cords and battery packs complicate matters, especially on one-man deployments. A completely self-contained 500,000 candlepower unit does not furnish as much light but it is more field practical.

Smaller lights mounted directly on weapons should be rugged, reliable, and shockproof. The size and brightness of the unit have to be balanced against bulk. You want as much light as possible without making the rifle too cumbersome. The Surefire standard battery models work well as carbine forearm-mounted lights. The rechargeable models are not recommended because regular batteries are more field practical. I do not recommend mounting lights to the rifle barrel because it could affect zero; likewise, mounting lights directly to the scope is inadvisable because a shock delivered to the light could be transmitted to the scope.

Standard-duty lights, such as the 20,000-30,000 candlepower StreamLight and MagLite work well for close-to-midrange-target illumination.

A small, red lens light should be carried for post work, such as reading the logbook or making adjustments to the turret. The red light has a less adverse affect on your night vision.

Carry extra batteries for any equipment requiring them. You will need them eventually (this is Murphy's Law applied to batteries).

A white light on target, of course, betrays the position of the light, and it should

Practice preparing accurate field cards and then confirm your accuracy in live-fire training.

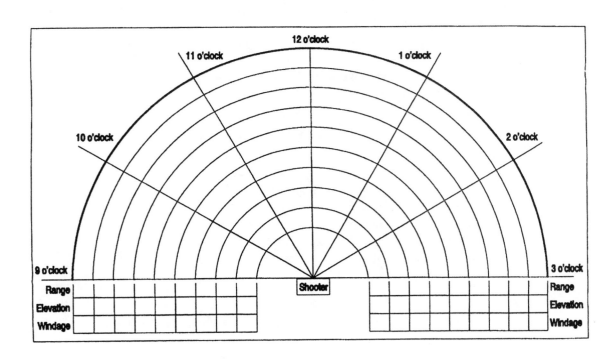

Wind flags provide valuable shot calculation information on the range. Watch the surrounding environment and the flag to see how the air movement affects both.

Matching camouflage to your surroundings is obviously the best course for covert operations.

not be used directly from, or in back of, the marksman's position when avoidable. The light should be directed from behind hard cover and only used intermittently unless remotely controlled and unmanned. The light operator should move from covered position to covered position between each illumination.

If an adversary is searching your area with a bright light, keep all reflective items covered and don't stare at the light. It will ruin your night vision, and any experienced night hunter can spot "eye glow" from hundreds of yards away.

Handling and manipulating the precision rifle safely are also very important. Getting the bolt down from the ready position and the shot off without disturbing the rifle requires training and practice.

A superior ghillie suit has well-frayed burlap or other movable material color coordinated to the operational environment. The front of the suit should feature heavy-duty skid panels and be well padded. An integral camelback water system is also a big plus.

If follow-up shots are a possibility, quick bolt-gun loading should be part of your training regimen. These operations must be second nature because they often must be done in darkness. Safe unloading is just as important because most situations end without a shot being fired, and the chamber will have to be cleared. Improper rifle manipulation and the resulting unintentional discharge could not only cause injuries, but also escalate an already tense situation.

You must develop field skills practical to your most frequently encountered environment. Applying proper camouflage for rural and urban use, entering and exiting hide locations, establishing field shooting positions, positioning yourself respective to wind and angles, determining target coverage angles, standardizing communications, detecting booby traps, remaining effective in inclement weather, and using cover and concealment should all be addressed in your training.

Operations in extreme climates require special considerations in more than just camouflage techniques. The precision marksman must be equipped to overcome the elements of his environment to perform effectively.

Marksmen expected to operate in near-Arctic conditions should train in similar conditions. Extreme cold weather requires the shooter to have clothing and equipment suitable to operate comfortably and reliably. Static positions require cold-weather clothing to avoid hypothermia. Insulating ground mats, sleeping bags, Mickey Mouse boots, and hand warmers help to prevent the shooter from get-

Hunting can provide excellent training in stalking, land navigation, camouflage, moving targets, and terminal bullet effects. This Wyoming predator was taken on a 90-degree run at 135 yards with a fast-handling carbine.

ting numb and suffering the shakes. Cold-weather shooters must ensure that their weapons don't freeze up by using the correct cold-weather lubricant, or no lubricant at all. Safely dry-fire your weapon in position to ensure that the trigger group and striker are operating properly. Avoid taking your rifle in and out of warm environments when operating in cold conditions. Doing so can create moisture in the warm environment that will turn to ice after you return to the cold, possibly causing the weapon to freeze up and the scope lens to glaze over.

Dedicating a four-wheel-drive vehicle, such as the Chevrolet Suburban, as a shooting platform provides a climate-controlled environment in many situations. Another field-expedient, cold-weather option when camouflage is not a priority is to shoot across the passenger compartment of a patrol unit. You can open both doors and assume a prone position across the front seat, near the radio and heater.

Ghillie suits are a popular method of camouflage in environments where visible vegetation is available. Professionally designed suits can be effective under the right

You must also develop good loading and unloading skills with the bolt rifle. The rear portion of the barrel on this rifle is solid-bedded just in front of the action where the cartridge carrier is located. Do not allow objects to come in contact with your free-floated barrel. After your field movement, check the barrel channel around the free-floated barrel for any foreign matter that may put pressure on it.

Position selection is critical. Avoid back-lighting your position. Firing from a window position requires you to be back in the shadow of the room, rather than your shooting from the opening.

Fieldcraft training should include camouflage and stalking techniques, as well as positioning and target coverage. Urban stalking requires adaptation to the specific environment.

The field marksman should have developed data at his fingertips. Note the data or dope bag on this shooter's bag. The sling-mounted sling must be secured when position shooting.

conditions. Some considerations are heat exhaustion in hot climates, weight of the suit if the wearer falls in the water, flame resistance, and speed of application in hasty responses. Outdoor equipment suppliers have been offering lightweight oversuits of "living" vegetation that offer an expedient solution to a tactical marksman needing something quickly to cover a uniform.

Engaging moving targets is a skill that must be practiced regularly to develop proficiency. Point-lead methods work well on consistently moving, predictable targets. You should develop and test lead data for your individual rifle-ammo combination. Of course, different speeds, angles, and distances require different amounts of lead. A tactical scope reticle helps in making correct lead judgments. Quick darting movements are probably going to be more of the norm in tactical situations. Close-to-medium-range darting targets are best engaged with the quick-

A reliable handgun can be an extremely useful tool for unexpected encounters. Handgun carry in the old-style GI chest (tanker) holster allows quick deployment from the prone position and doesn't interfere with a ghillie suit.

handling carbine and a swing-through method, which requires training and experience. See chart on page 128.

Game hunting can provide a wealth of experience for a tactical marksman. You can learn to track moving targets with a scoped rifle by going after such fast-moving animals as jackrabbits, foxes, and coyotes. Herd hunting is also an opportunity to pick out your target and make the shot while it is in close proximity to other "no shoot" targets. When shooting a big-game animal out of a herd, you must consider all the nearby "no shoot" animals. Having only one tag for one type of animal will add to the pressure of the shot. Your bullet's performance can be evaluated by its impact as well.

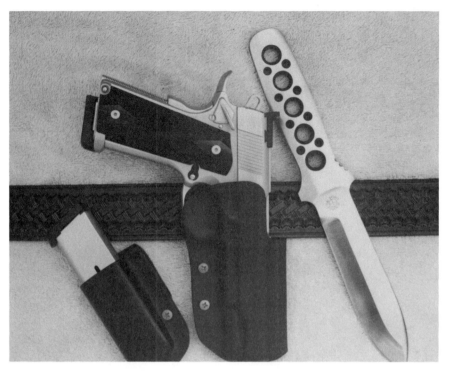

Stalking and camouflage techniques can also be tested in the game fields. Creatures of the wild normally have extremely sharp senses of smell and hearings. Prairie dog towns have an effective network of sentries and alert tones for warning the entire area of the presence of outsiders. These creatures provide effective and interesting stalking training. They do so much property damage that they are fair game in most areas. This gives you the opportunity to stalk, calculate, and make the shot on a target that is approximately 2 by 6 inches.

Calling such animals as coyotes and foxes lets you test your camouflage on some of the most wary animals in the world. If your hide spot is not compatible with your surroundings, or if you smell funny or

State-of-the-art Kydex holsters and accessory pouches are well-suited to the tactical marksman. The holster pictured is waterproof, rotproof, and form-retaining.

have poor noise discipline or patience, these creatures will not give you a second chance—or even a first shot.

A note of caution for shooters in the western United States: there are verified outbreaks of bubonic plague in some predators and prairie dogs. Don't handle these carcasses without precautions, especially if you have any open cuts. Avoiding rattlesnakes and ticks that might infect you with Rocky Mountain Spotted Fever should be enough to keep you busy without having to deal with the plague!

Tactics acquired from team paintball or Simunition training can be beneficial to the countersniper as well. Provided that it is kept realistic, this kind of training will provide head-to-head comparison of tactical skills. Your training should cover all areas that you can reasonably expect to encounter in your environment.

A custom M1911-style auto pistol is an excellent support weapon for the tactical marksman.

Rifle **10**
Maintenance

NONCORROSIVE PRIMERS, JACKETED BULLETS, WEATHERPROOF STOCKS, AND STAINLESS steel seem to make some shooters believe that rifle maintenance is a thing of the past. It is not. A clean rifle, especially the bore, is one of the main reasons that precision rifles can shoot 1/8-inch groups at 100 yards, which benchrest shooters do regularly. One of the most important lessons we can learn from precision shooters is proper rifle cleaning.

Each time a round is fired, residue is left from the burning of the primer and powder. As the bullet passes through the bore, copper fouling is left behind. This happens on every shot. If the fouling is not removed it will diminish accuracy.

The number of rounds fired between cleanings is often debated from one extreme to the other. Some shooters want to shoot only one bullet down their bore before cleaning, while others think the bore should never be cleaned because it may change the group.

Fouling first builds up in front of the chamber. Repeated firing of bullets over this buildup will turn it into a substance harder than the barrel itself. Allowing the residue to build up and "iron" onto the barrel metal causes irreparable damage to the barrel. It cannot be removed without damaging the bore or shortening the barrel to remove the affected area.

A buildup as small as .002 to .003 of an inch will act as a bullet sizer each time a bullet passes over it. Because the area is smaller in diameter than the rest of the barrel, it acts as a constriction point. Top match-grade barrels have bore tolerances of .0001 to 0002 inch throughout their length. This means that the fouling-sized bullet will fit more loosely in the rest of the barrel after passing over the fouling sizer. This will, of course, result in a loss of accuracy.

I recommend firing no more than 10 rounds through a precision rifle before bore cleaning.

If you routinely practice at one range, you should set up a padded rifle vise or vises at the range to complete this chore. The vise should be form-cut to suit the forearm width of your rifle and be padded to protect the stock. The vise should hold the rifle with the muzzle angled down to allow solvent to run down and out, rather than back into the action and bedding.

A padded rifle vise simplifies rifle maintenance. Notice the pressure-relief ports in the bottom of this rifle's bolt.

Your cleaning rod should be a top-quality, one-piece unit. Sectional cleaning rods are not suitable for precision rifle cleaning (except in true field emergencies). The off-center joints of steel cleaning rods can scuff and scratch a premium bore. You should get the best quality sectional cleaning rod for your field pack if no other rod is practical. In situations where you stuff your muzzle in the mud or get a case stuck in the chamber, such a rod will allow you to get "shootable" again. A full-length drag bag, or hard case in the field, will allow you to carry a one-piece rod without problem.

Whether to use stainless steel or coated cleaning rods is often a subject for debate. Those in favor of stainless steel believe that coated rods can get foreign material impregnated into them, causing barrel damage by acting as a lap (the same reason aluminum rods are bad). The coated rod users say they don't want to use something as hard as the barrel to clean it (the same reason stainless steel brushes are not recommended).

I hold with the theory of using something softer than the metal you are cleaning to avoid peening or galling problems. This means a clean, top-quality, one-piece, coated cleaning rod. Keep the rod surface clean, and do not let it become impregnated with foreign material. Wearing out the coating and replacing a cleaning rod is cheaper than a new match barrel. Top-quality, vinyl-coated, one-piece rods are available from Dewey and Parker-Hale These rods are available from most precision-shooting outlets.

Flannel patches and pointed jag should fit snugly in the bore of your particular caliber. Pointed jags are preferable to the eyelet styles because they evenly push the patch through the bore and drop them out the muzzle. The eyelet styles are uneven and, if pulled back through, can pull residue back into the bore. Don't pull dirty patches back through the bore. Always check your bore for obstructions after cleaning—jags or sectional rods can come apart, and patches can be left in the bore.

To find the best cleaning solvent you could spend days reading all the labels and claims of the various brands on the market today. I have narrowed the field to two choices (as of this writing): Shooter's Choice works well as a regular bore cleaner, and Sweets 7.62 is a more aggressive solvent that attacks seriously fouled bores. Using Shooter's Choice for regular cleaning and doing another cleaning every fifth cleaning with Sweet's should keep things clean. Using any of the abrasive cleaners with lapping or cutting action is not recommended. Some solvents require interaction with oxygen. This means that using a barrel plug and soaking the bore overnight will not work. Soaking the barrel with some of the aggressive compounds will pit the barrel. *Read the instructions thoroughly.* The Foul-Out electric bore cleaner also works in shop applications.

Good solvent should be a part of every shooter's cleaning gear.

Bore guides serve to align the cleaning rods with the bore. Don't clean without one. They will also keep the solvent from dripping into the trigger mechanism and gumming it beyond proper function. Sloppy solvent handling will also drip into your bedding material and may turn it into mush. Install the bore guide in the action after removing the bolt. Better bore guides have a rubber O-ring or other seal at the front end. This O-ring seals the chamber so that solvent won't leak back into the action. Make sure the ring stays on the bore guide when you remove it; if it becomes stuck in the chamber during removal, it may become a dangerous barrel obstruction if not detected.

A top-quality bore guide and one-piece cleaning rod are essential for precision rifle maintenance.

The bore guide should have a minimal cleaning rod hole to prevent any bending of the rod while cleaning. The bore guide should also have some type of lever that locks into the bolt handle cut in the stock to secure it in place while stroking the rod.

Without a bore guide, the cleaning rod can bow and damage the lands just forward of the lead. It should be carried, even in the field, with your other cleaning supplies.

A cleaning regimen should conform to the following procedure:

1. Unload the chamber and magazine (double safety check).
2. Close your scope covers.
3. Secure the rifle in a cleaning vise or on its bipod with the muzzle lower than the action.
4. Remove the bolt and install the bore guide.
5. Cover the buttstock with a cloth to avoid solvent contamination.
6. Place a fitted, solvent saturated patch on the jag and pass it through the bore. When time permits, give the barrel 5 to 10 minutes or so to soak.
7. In the unfortunate event you get a patch stuck in the bore, do not force it or you could damage the bore. Sticking a properly sized patch usually means the patch and bore were too dry upon insertion. To loosen things up, tip the muzzle up and run some solvent down the bore to saturate the patch. Squeeze-bottle applicators work best. Once it is soaked, you should be able to push the patch through easily.
8. Install a top-quality brass brush with a bronze core on your cleaning rod. Squeeze some solvent onto your brush; do not dip the brush into a bottle of solvent because it will contaminate the container of solvent. Run the brush through the bore at least one full stroke, forward and back, for each round fired. Do not attempt to reverse the stroke while the brush is in the bore, only after it comes out the muzzle or chamber. Apply a small amount of additional solvent to your brush two to three times during this procedure: this means things should be wet, but not excessively.
9. Patch the bore out until the last patch out is clean and dry. When using Sweet's Solvent, the patches will probably come out green. This is an indication of copper fouling being removed. After using a brass brush with Sweet's Solvent, throw it away.
10. After the bore is patched clean, remove the bore guide. Clean and dry the chamber. A large-caliber bronze pistol brush followed by a chamber mop on a pistol rod works fine. A twisting, clockwise motion works well when cleaning the chamber. During the final passes, the mop can be coated lightly with an evaporating degreaser, such as Gunscrubber, to make sure it is completely dry.
11. If you plan to use your brass brush again, blow it off with Gunscrubber and compressed air, or it will deteriorate. Keep the brush housed in its clear plastic tube to avoid its picking up any grit. Then run one more clean, dry patch all the way through the bore.
12. Clean the bolt body, bolt face, and bolt-locking lugs. Clean the locking lug recesses inside the action. A special-action cleaning tool with swabs is best for this job. The bolt face should be completely free of dirt, brass shavings, and any oil or solvent that could affect cartridge primers. The rear of the bolt's locking lugs should receive a very light coating of nonfreezable grease. Also apply light grease to the rear of the bolt body where it cams against the receiver to prevent galling during operation. (The bolt handle should be left in its unlocked position if the rifle is going to be stored for a substantial period to eliminate any metal stresses from tight locking lug-to-action fit.)

Most shooters end their bore-cleaning process at this point, relying on the first shot out of a cold barrel to be "on." And this is quite likely for a properly built and maintained rifle, but for a duty rifle, I prefer to do a zero confirmation after bore cleaning. The rifle that is going back into on-duty status has to be zeroed on the first shot out. Any solvent residue, patch cloth, or unknown variables could cause a live-fire cold shot to be off.

If for no other reason than the elimination of variables and instilling confidence, you should always do a zero confirmation before putting a rifle back into on-duty status. This means that your cleaning has to be done at the range and the zero confirmed before you leave. Following a thorough cleaning procedure, firing a

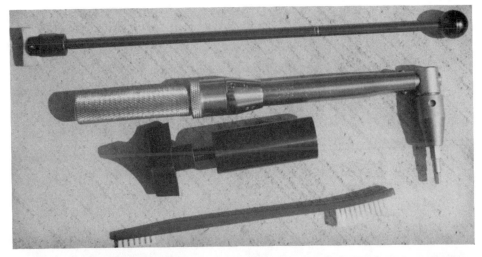

Use proper cleaning supplies for maintaining your precision rifle. (Below) Notice the indicator marks placed on the stock screws after they have been properly torqued.

three-shot confirmation group will remove all doubt of the rifle's POI.

For long-term storage, the rifle and bore should be clean and lightly oiled. It will have to be completely cleaned and the zero confirmed after it is taken out of storage and before it is put "on call" for duty use.

More substantial cleaning procedures are required if the rifle has been exposed to severe conditions.

Stock removal and bolt disassembly should be accomplished only by the educated marksman or gunsmith with the right tools. The minimum of tools required for the task are a torque wrench, bolt disassembly tool, and small hand tools. Screws should be marked after being secured so that you can visually check later for loosening. If you are unsure of the procedures, get professional guidance. You should not allow anyone who is not a competent gunsmith to attempt to tune or disassemble your rifle.

Your scope should be waterproof and fogproof. No disassembly outside the factory is recommended. Protect the lenses with scope caps and clean them only as required. Any cleaning should only be done with proper cleaning supplies, which are best obtained from a camera supply store or the scope companies themselves.

Anytime any changes or modifications are made, such as stock removal or scope or trigger adjustments, you must return to the range and confirm the safety, accuracy, and zero of your rifle before putting it back on call.

Periodic inspections and accuracy updates, such as rebarrelling, by a competent gunsmith should be figured into your maintenance program.

Specify whatever metal surface protection you want, such as hard-chroming, when ordering your rifle. This will provide a protective base, over which you may apply camouflage. In any event, you should care for your equipment meticulously and pack silica gel with it to avoid moisture buildup.

Sample Field Data Book

FIELD DATA BOOK
(SAMPLE)

Weapon _____ S/N _____

Scope _____

Ammo _____

Ammo Lot # _____

Shooter _____

Date _____

Current Ammo Lot # in use

#	Date Issued	Date Data Confirmed
_____	_____	_____
_____	_____	_____
_____	_____	_____
_____	_____	_____
_____	_____	_____

Trajectory Data

Zero Range __100 yards__

Yards		Required Hold or Up Clicks
25	_____	Hold
50	_____	Hold
75	_____	Hold
100	_____	Zero
150	_____	_____
200	_____	_____
250	_____	_____
300	_____	_____
350	_____	_____
400	_____	_____
450	_____	_____
500	_____	_____
550	_____	_____
600	_____	_____
650	_____	_____
700	_____	_____
750	_____	_____
800	_____	_____
850	_____	_____
900	_____	_____
950	_____	_____
1,000	_____	_____

Wind Drift 10 mph 90° Cross

Ammo _____

Bullet _____

Velocity _____

Ballistic Coefficient _____

Inches Drift

100	_____	_____
150	_____	_____
200	_____	_____
250	_____	_____
300	_____	_____
350	_____	_____
400	_____	_____
450	_____	_____
500	_____	_____
550	_____	_____
600	_____	_____
650	_____	_____
700	_____	_____
750	_____	_____
800	_____	_____
850	_____	_____
900	_____	_____
950	_____	_____
1,000	_____	_____

RIFLE LOG

COLD BORE SHOT: CALL   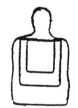   HIT   

_____ YARD TARGET

RANGE	RIFLE/SCOPE		DATE	ELEVATION		WINDAGE	
				USED	CORRECT	USED	CORRECT

AMMUNITION	LIGHT	MIRAGE	TEMP	HOUR

LIGHT   **WIND**

(LIGHT clock face: 12, 9, 3, 6)

(WIND clock face: 12, 9, 3, 6)

VELOCITY   DIRECTION

AMMUNITION & LOT NUMBER _____

ADDITIONAL:

Sample Cold-Shot Target

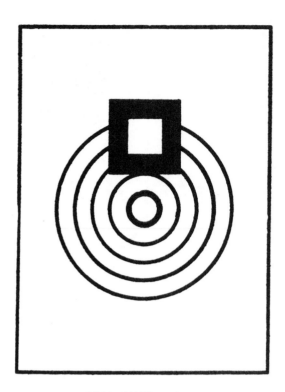

COLD SHOT TARGET

Temperature ——————— Rifle S/N ——————
Date——————— Load —————————
Shooter ——————— Distance —————
Location ——————— Scope ——————
Lot # ——————— Position ——————

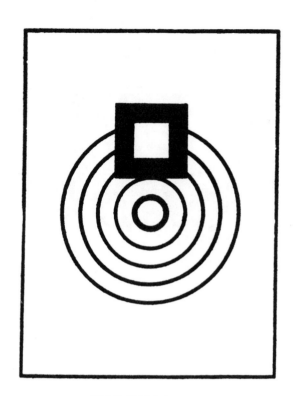

COLD SHOT TARGET

Temperature ——————— Rifle S/N ——————
Date——————— Load —————————
Shooter ——————— Distance —————
Location ——————— Scope ——————
Lot # ——————— Position ——————

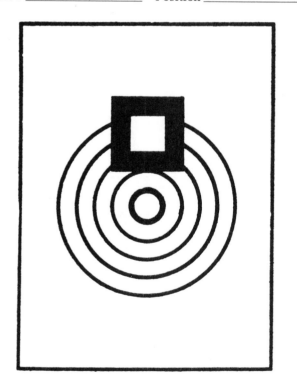

COLD SHOT TARGET

Temperature ——————— Rifle S/N ——————
Date——————— Load —————————
Shooter ——————— Distance —————
Location ——————— Scope ——————
Lot # ——————— Position ——————

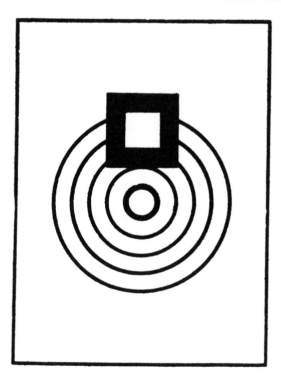

COLD SHOT TARGET

Temperature ——————— Rifle S/N ——————
Date——————— Load —————————
Shooter ——————— Distance —————
Location ——————— Scope ——————
Lot # ——————— Position ——————

List of Suppliers and Training Schools

Suppliers

Professional-grade cold-weather clothing:
Dave Pacanowsky
W.L. Gore and Associates, Inc.
297 Blue Ball Road
Elkton, MD 21921

Custom-loaded ammunition:
Vulpes Ventures, Inc.
Fox Cartridge Divison
P.O. Box 1363
Bolingbrook, IL 60440-7363

Ghillie suits and drag bags:
Concealment Concepts/Jim Grzech
5101 Ashley Phosphate Rd.
Suite 104, #275/TM
North Charleston, SC 29418

Training Schools

D & L Sports/S.A.T.A.
Dave Lauck
P.O. Box 651
Gillette, WY 82717

John Plaster
1900 E. Shore Drive, #3
St. Paul, MN 55109

STTU
Mark Longsdale
P.O. Box 491261
Los Angeles, CA 90049

Thunder Ranch
Clint Smith
HCR1, Box 53
Mt. Home, TX 78058

Glossary

Accuracy—the firearm's ability to shoot consistently where aimed; the measure of a bullet's precision.

Action—the part of a firearm where ammunition is loaded, fired, and unloaded.

Air resistance—the composition of matter in the atmosphere that serves to retard the forward motion of a projectile by slowing it down. Ballistic efficiency is the relative ability of a bullet to overcome this resistance.

Annealing—heating a metal to soften it. As it applies to shooting, a process that softens brass case necks to prevent cracking from repeated reloading.

Anvil—the pointed portion of a primer against which the explosive compound is driven by a firing pin, striker, or hammer, causing detonation.

AO—adjustable objective.

AP—armor piercing.

Backstop—an impact point that will not allow bullet penetration.

Ball powder—spherical, double-based powder originally developed by Olin Industries for the military. It is said to retard throat erosion.

Ballistic coefficient (BC)—the index of a projectile's ability to overcome resistance in flight relative to the performance of a standard projectile used to compute ballistic tables.

Ballistics—the study of projectiles in motion. Exterior ballistics deals with the performance of a projectile after it leaves the gun; interior ballistics deals with events inside a gun, from primer ignition to the projectile exiting the muzzle. Terminal ballistics deals with bullet performance upon target impact.

Barrel flutes—grooves milled lengthwise into the barrel's outer surface to aid cooling, reduce weight, and add rigidity.

Base—attachment for scope rings; can be one or two piece.

BC—ballistic coefficient.

Bearing surface—the portion of a projectile that contacts the lands and grooves as it passes through a barrel.

Bedding—a manner in which the barrel and action are fitted to the stock.

Belted case—a cartridge case that has a raised area around the base and ahead of the extraction groove. These cases headspace on the belted band. (See Headspace.)

Benchrest—competition shot over a solid table; provides greater accuracy.

Berdan primer—primers having no anvil, but which use a protrusion from the top of the primer pocket to cause ignition. Common in European cartridges.

Bipod—two-point rifle support.

Boat-tail—a tapered bullet base commonly found on military and match bullets.

Bolt—the part on a rifle or shotgun that houses the striker and the case extractor, and rotates to lock the cartridge or shell in the chamber.

Bolt action—a weapon that is manually reloaded by use of a bolt.

Bolt thrust—force against the bolt face, caused by the pressure of burning powder.

Bore sight—to align the sights of a firearm by looking through the barrel. A term commonly used when referring to the use of a collimator.

Bore—inside of the barrel through which the bullet travels.

Boxer primer—a primer using a self-contained anvil and a single flashhole. Common in U.S. cartridges.

Brass—copper and zinc alloy used to make cartridge cases and bullet jackets. Also a common name for the cases themselves.

Breech—the loading end of the barrel.

BT—boat-tail.

Bullet—projectile.

Burning rate—the speed at which a smokeless powder burns. Affected by size of granules, amount and nature of deterrent coating, and perforation.

Caliber—the diameter of a bullet or projectile expressed in millimeters or decimals of an inch. Also, the diameter of a bore expressed similarly.

Canister—a container of powder; usually in a standard size or weight.

Cannelure—crimp or lubricant groove on a bullet.

Cartridge—a complete, self-contained unit of ammunition.

Case hardening—a process whereby the outer layer of iron-based metal objects is strengthened.

Case-length gauge—a device used to measure cartridge-case length.

Case-neck brush—a tool used to lubricate and clean the inside of a case prior to reloading.

Case trimmer—a device, either electrical or hand power, used to shorten cases, usually rifle cases, lengthened by repeated firing and reloading.

Case—(cartridge case) a metal, plastic, or paper that holds all of the components of a round of ammunition. Configurations include bottle-necked, tapered, or straight cases.

Cast bullet—a bullet made by pouring molten lead into a mold.

Centerfire—a cartridge that has the primer located in the center of the base of the case. Usually reloadable.

Chamber—the breech portion of a firearm that contains the cartridge.

Chamfering-deburring tool—a device used to bevel the inside of a cartridge-case mouth. Removes burrs and facilitates reloading.

Channel—the groove cut in the fore-end of the stock to accept the barrel.

Charge—the amount of powder loaded into a cartridge case. Usually measured in grains.

Chronograph—an instrument that measures velocity of a projectile. Projectiles are timed while in flight over a known distance; this distance, divided by the time of flight, is the velocity of the projectile. Usually expressed in feet per second (fps).

Clicks—units of measure used in scope adjustment.

Cold shot—the first shot fired from a weapon without warmup or spotter shots.

Collimator—an optical device inserted in the bore and used to align telescopic sights with the bore.

Combustion—the burning of powder in a cartridge that produces heat and gas.

Components—ingredients necessary to load a cartridge; usually, the case, primer, powder, and bullet.

Compressed charge—a charge of powder that is compacted in the cartridge case by deep bullet-seating depth.

Copper crusher—a device consisting of a copper alloy cylinder of known density and exact dimensions, used in measuring chamber pressure. An index of pressure is determined by the changes in the length of the cylinder, and a table is used to calculate pressure in pounds per square inch.

Copper—a metal used in such alloys as brass and bronze.

Core—the center portion of a jacketed bullet.

Creep—movement in trigger prior to discharge.

Crimp remover—a device used to remove the crimping flange on an empty cartridge case using a crimped primer.

Crimp—the fold in the mouth of a cartridge case that holds the bullet in place.

Crimped primer—a flange indentation used in military ammunition to secure the primer in the primer pocket. This helps seal the primer in the case and prevent primer setback upon firing. This crimp must be removed before reloading.

Cross hairs—thin crossed lines used as an aiming device inside a scope.

Crown—machining of the muzzle end of the barrel to precise dimensions.

Deburring tool—a device to remove metal burrs from the mouths of newly trimmed cases.

Decap—deprime; to remove the primer.

Deflection—a change in path of the bullet because of wind or passage through a medium.

Deterrent coating—the combustion-controlling chemical coating used on smokeless powder particles to produce desired burning characteristics.

Die—in bullet manufacturing, a tool that extrudes lead wire, draws bullet jackets, or swages bullets or cores. In reloading, a tool that sizes cases or seats bullets.

Doping (wind)—estimating wind effect.

Double-base powder—smokeless powder made with both nitrocellulose and nitroglycerine.

Drift—the deviation of a projectile from the line of departure because of rotation or wind.

Drop compensator—a sight adjustment to correct for bullet drop at various distances.

Drop—the distance a projectile falls because of gravity measured from the zero point.

Dry-fire—aiming and firing the weapon without live ammunition.

Duplex—wide posts converging in a fine cross hair.

Elevation—the vertical sight adjustment that brings the point of aim up or down to intersect with the point of impact.

Energy—the capacity for doing work; transferring force. Spoken of in ballistics as muzzle energy or remaining energy. Measured in foot pounds.

Erosion—the bore or throat wear in a firearm from the effects of hot gases and friction.

Exterior ballistics—the study of a projectile's flight after exiting the muzzle.

Extractor—a hook to remove cartridge from chamber.

Extruded primer—the pronounced flow of primer metal ("cratering") around the striker or firing pin of a firearm. An indication of excessive pressure.

Extrusion—a process in which material is forced through a die of the desired shape.

Eye relief—distance from the shooter's eye to the rear of the scope.

Factory load—commercially manufactured ammunition.

Fire-form—to re-form a cartridge case by firing it in a chamber of different dimensions.

Firing pin—part of a weapon's mechanism that strikes the primer.

Flake powder—a thin, flat disk-type smokeless powder, generally very fast burning.

Flash hole—the hole or holes from the primer pocket through the web of a centerfire case through which the primer flame passes to ignite the powder.

Flat point—a bullet style characterized by its blunt point and designed especially for rifles with tubular magazines.

Floating—removing all contact points between barrel and stock.

FMJ—full-metal jacket.

Foot-pound (ft.-lb.)—a unit of work; the energy required to lift one pound one foot.

Fore-end—the forward section of the stock used for weapon support.

Fouling—the buildup of copper and powder residue in the bore.

FPS—feet per second.

Freebore—an unrifled portion of the bore in front of the chamber. (See Chamber, Leade.)

Full-metal jacket (FMJ)—a bullet whose jacket is open only at the rear. FMJs for hunting are nonexpanding and generally used on thick-skinned animals. Full-metal jacket or full-patch bullets are also used by the military.

Galling—a roughness on the surface of two metals created from friction as the surfaces are "rubbed" together.

Gas—the vaporous form of a substance capable of expanding indefinitely to fill its container. Gases are a product of the combustion of gunpowder and expand to propel the projectile down the bore.

Ghillie wrap—a highly camouflaged cloak used for sniper concealment. Can be a complete suit.

Go/No-go gauges—also minimum-maximum gauges. Standard measuring devices to indicate proper headspace in a firearm, proper cartridge length, etc.

Grain—a unit of weight; 437.5 grains equal 1 ounce; 7,000 grains equal 1 pound.

Grooves—swaged impressions or cuts spiraled through a bore to rotate projectiles.

Group—the distribution of bullets on a target fired with a single aiming point and sight setting. Group size is expressed as the distance between centers of the farthest holes and is most easily determined by measuring the extreme spread from outside to outside and subtracting one bullet diameter.

Handload—hand-manufactured ammunition.

Handstop—a device attached to a weapon's fore-end to prevent the hand from sliding forward.

Handloading—loading individual cartridges with hand tools.

Hangfire—an inordinate delay between the striking of the primer and powder ignition.

Headspace—the fit of a cartridge in a chamber measured as the distance from breech face to that part of the chamber that stops the case's forward movement. Insufficient headspace hinders complete chambering; excessive headspace permits case stretching or separation.

Hold-off—the distance aimed to the right or left of the target to compensate for wind or deflection.

Hold-over—the distance a shooter must raise his point of aim to be on target when his firearm is zeroed in at a lesser distance.

Hold-under—distance aimed below target to compensate for a rising projectile.

Hollowpoint (HP)—bullet with hollow cavity in the tip.

HP—hollowpoint.

Ignition—the powder "lighting" (igniting) process.

Interior ballistics—the study of forces operating prior to the bullet exiting the muzzle.

Jacket—the copper covering of the lead core of the bullet.

Keyhole—the imprint of an unstabilized bullet on a target.

Lands—high points in rifling of barrel.

Leade—freebore; the unrifled area immediately in front of the chamber. In most firearms it is quite short.

Line of departure—a projection of the axis of the bore from which a projectile is fired.

Line of sight—the straight line through the sights of a firearm to the aiming point.

Loading block—a useful accessory for holding cartridge cases for reloading.

Loading density—a volume ratio of powder charge to case capacity.

Locking lugs—bolt projections that fit mating recesses in the receiver to secure the bolt from rearward movement when a cartridge is fired.

Log—a detailed record of weapon's life.

Loophole—a hole cut to conceal but allow shooting.

Lot—a group of ammunition assembled with the same components.

Lube pad—a lubricant-impregnated stamp pad on which cases are rolled before sizing.

Lubricant—a substance to preserve metal and reduce friction.

Magazine—separate or integral part of a weapon that contains additional ammunition ready to fire.

Magnum—a cartridge or firearm of greater power and capacity than earlier standards in the same caliber.

Mercuric primer—a primer whose explosive mixture contains mercuric compounds that will attack metal after firing.

Metal fouling—the depositing of bullet or jacket metal in the bore of a firearm, a process detrimental to best accuracy.

Midrange trajectory—the highest vertical distance of a bullet above the line of sight at a point approximately halfway from the muzzle to the target.

Mil—an angular measurement equal to 3.375 MOA. A mil subtends 1 yard at 1,000 yards.

Minute of angle (MOA)—a unit of angular measurement approximated as one inch to 100 yards (actually equal to 1.047 inches per 100 yards).

Misfire—a round that fails to fire when struck by the firing pin.

MOA—minute of angle.

Mounts—refers to rings and bases for scope installation.

Mushroom—to expand.

Muzzle velocity—the speed of a projectile at the muzzle of a firearm.

Muzzle blast—the release of gas from the muzzle following the bullet's departure from the barrel. It always produces noise and is often accompanied by light called muzzle flash.

Muzzle energy—foot pounds of energy of a projectile at the muzzle of a firearm.

Muzzle—the point at which the projectile leaves the barrel.

Neck size—to bring the neck of a case back to its original dimensions to hold a new bullet. Cases fired in the same chamber need neck sizing (resizing) only.

Neck turn—the process of making neck wall thickness uniform from the outside of the case.

Neck—the upper portion of a cartridge case that grips the bullet, expands on firing to release it, and in reloading must be resized to hold a new bullet.

Neck ream—the process of removing metal from the inside of the neck of a case.

No-shoot target—a hostage or bystander target used in training.

Noncorrosive—primers made without potassium chlorate, a chemical that when oxidized forms a water-attracting salt that induces bore rusting.

O-press—a very strong type of reloading press with a continuous frame.

Ogive—the curve of a bullet's forward portion.

Parallax—the condition that exists when the reticle of a scope does not lie exactly on the image plane. When this optical error exists, changes of eye position will move the position of the reticle relative to the object sighted.

Patch—small piece of cloth used to clean the bore.

Pierced primer—a primer whose cup is completely perforated by the striker. Such a condition permits powder gases to escape rearward into the action.

POA—point of aim.

Point of aim—point on the target where the cross hairs are positioned.

POI—point of impact.

Point of impact—the point where the bullet strikes the target.

Powder measure—a reloadiing device designed to throw uniform powder charges.

Powder scale—a measuring device to weigh powder.

Powder trickler—a reloading accessory to drop minute quantities of powder to facilitate precise loading.

Powder—propellant material used in most firearms.

Pressure—force per unit area; measured in interior ballistics terms of pounds per square inch.

Primer pocket swaging—removing the crimp in primer pocket of a military case by using a punch and base set. Crimps may also be removed by reaming.

Primer leak—gases that have escaped between the primer and the primer pocket wall because of excess pressure.

Primer pocket—the recess in the base of the cartridge to accept the primer.

Primer tool—a tool designed specifically for priming.

Primer—the small cup filled with detonating mixture that is used to ignite the propellant powder.

Projectile—a missile in flight.

Prone—the shooting position where the shooter is lying flat.

Propellant—the powder burned to propel a projectile.

Protruding primer—a primer that, after firing, backs out beyond flush with the case head, normally a result of excess headspace or a low pressure load.

Rail—an adjustable insert in fore-end of the weapon to accept hand stop or sling.

Range finder—a system designed to estimate range of target.

Range—the distance to an intended target.

Receiver—that portion of a firearm that holds the barrel and houses the bolt and firing mechanism.

Recoil lug—a heavy metal protrusion beneath the front of the action to transfer recoil to the stock.

Recoil pad—a rubber pad attached to rear of stock to protect shooter's shoulder and prevent slippage.

Recoil—the rearward motion or "kick" of a gun on firing. Recoil in shooting is the practical effect of Newton's Third Law of Motion: for every action there is an opposite and equal reaction.

Reload—hand-loaded ammunition.

Reloading press—a tool for reforming cartridge cases and seating bullets in cartridge reloading.

Remaining energy—a projectile's energy in foot-pounds at a given range.

Remaining velocity—a projectile's velocity in feet per second at a given range.

Resizing die—the reloading die which reforms cartridge cases to proper dimensions.

Reticle—the system of cross hairs, fine lines, or dots in the focus of a telescope.

Retina—light-sensitive layer at the back of the eye.

Rifle—a long weapon with a grooved bore designed to make the bullet spin.

Rifling—the grooves within the barrel, designed to spin the bullet and increase stability.

Rimfire—a cartridge discharged by a strike to the rim.

Rimless case—a cartridge case whose base flange is the same diameter as the case head. The groove ahead of the rim permits extraction.

Rimless—a cartridge whose rim is the same diameter as its body.

Rimmed case—a case with a flange on its base. This rim is used for both extraction and as a means of headspacing the cartridge.

Rimmed—a cartridge whose rim is wider than its body.

Rings—devices used to support the scope.

Rotation—the spin of a projectile imparted to it by the rifling. The faster the twist of the rifling or the higher the velocity, the faster the rotation.

Round-nose—a bullet with a blunt rounded tip.

Round—a complete cartridge.

Safety—a mechanical device to prevent weapon firing.

Scope—an optical sighting device.

Scope caps—dust covers protecting elevation and windage

Scope covers—scope covers to protect scope lenses.

Seating depth—the length of a bullet seated inside the cartridge case.

Seating die—a reloading die that inserts the bullet in the neck of the cartridge case.

Sectional density—the ratio of a bullet's weight in pounds to the square of its diameter in inches. Bullets of the same shape but with more weight in relation to their diameter retain their velocity and energy better.

Semiautomatic—a weapon system that automatically reloads itself but only fires once on each trigger pull.

Semi-rimmed case—a cartridge case with a rim slightly larger than the body diameter. The extraction groove is not as deeply cut in this type of case as in a rimless case.

Shell holder—the cartridge case holder on a reloading press or other tool.

Shock wave—the atmospheric disturbance produced by a supersonic projectile.

Shock—the transference of the kinetic energy of a bullet to animal tissue or other

Shoulder—the projection of a bottlenecked cartridge case from the neck to the case body; the point at which the head of a projectile joins the cylindrical rear portion.

Sight—a device for aiming a firearm; the process of aiming.

Sighting in—firing a rifle or pistol to determine its point of impact at a specified range and to adjust the sights so that the point of impact has the desired relationship to the point of aim.

Sling—leather strap used to increase stability while shooting.

Smokeless powder—a high-energy propellant used in small arms projectiles.

Soft-point—a bullet with an exposed lead tip designed for increased expansion.

Solvent—chemical compound to remove fouling from the bore.

Spin—the rotation of a projectile imparted by the rifling in a firearm's bore.

Stabilize—to rotate a projectile around its longitudinal axis rapidly enough to keep it point on in flight.

Stock—the wood or fiberglass part of a weapon system designed to support the action and barrel and facilitate shooting.

Stuck case remover—a device to remove stuck cases in a reloading die.

Swage—to form with pressure.

SWAT—special weapons and tactics.

Swivels—attachment points for sling to stock.

Terminal ballistics—the study of the effect of a bullet's impact on the target.

Terminal velocity—the speed of the bullet upon impact with the target.

Throat—leade or freebore; the unrifled portion of the bore immediately in front of the chamber. Usually very short.

Time of flight—the time it takes a projectile to cover a given distance.

Torque—the turning force applied to screws or bolts.

Tracer—a phosphorescent projectile visible at night.

Trajectory—the flight path of a projectile.

Tripod—a three-point rifle support.

Twist—the rate of spiral of the grooves of a rifle barrel expressed in length of barrel per revolution.

Varmint—a bird or animal commonly considered a pest.

Velocity—the speed of a projectile expressed as distance per unit time.

Web—the thickness of the solid portion a brass cartridge case between the primer pocket and the case interior. Also the wall thickness of tubular powder.

Wildcat—a noncommercial cartridge design.

Wind deflection—the lateral deflection of a bullet caused by a crosswind.

Windage—horizontal (lateral) sight adjustment.

X—power of scope magnification.

Yaw—normally, a situation where a bullet rotates on its axis at a small angle to the line of flight.

Zero—to set the sights so that the point of impact is identical to the point of aim.

About the Author

DAVE LAUCK IS A VETERAN POLICE OFFICER WITH EXTENSIVE EXPERIENCE IN PRAC-tical firearms, firearm instruction, gunsmithing, SWAT, police counter-sniping training, special investigations, and patrolling. He is a certified armorer whose skills have earned him recognition as one of America's top five pis-tolsmiths and induction into Club 100, a group of America's top gunsmiths. He is a founding life member of the 1911 Society, a life member of the NRA, and a member of the American Gunsmithing Association.

Lauck is an NRA-certified handgun, shotgun, and long-range rifle instructor. He holds expert firearms ratings and has received numerous awards in competitive practical shooting, including the following: team captain at the 1991 World Championship Tactical Match, first place in the 1990 World Championship Tactical Rifle Event, top 10-percent finisher in overall Three-Gun World Championship in 1990, first place in the 600-meter NRA Long-Range Rifle Instructor Shoot-Off in 1988, first-place SAA Countersniper Shootoff in 1987, SDHP Two-Gun Combat Match Police Champion in 1986, Northwest Regional Champion in 1985, and Wyoming Tactical Division winner in 1995.

He is the founder of D & L Sports Custom Firearms, Inc. and Small Arms Training Academy (S.A.T.A.) in Gillette, Wyoming. He teaches his performance-proven shooting principles to law enforcement and military personnel and other qualified individuals. For a D & L catalog or an application to S.A.T.A., please send $8 to the address below.

D & L SPORTS
Custom Firearms and Small Arms Training Academy
P.O. Box 651
Gillette, WY 82717-0651

DATE DUE

GAYLORD			PRINTED IN U.S.A.